CONQUEST & OVERLORD

The story of the Bayeux Tapestry and the Overlord Embroidery

by
Brian Jewell

Illustrated by Philip Giggle

ARCO PUBLISHING INC.

The Overlord Embroidery is on
permanent display at the Headquarters
of Whitbread & Co. Ltd
in Chiswell Street, London, E.C.1.

Produced by MIDAS BOOKS
© 1981 Text BRIAN JEWELL
© 1957 Bayeux Tapestry Pictures PHAIDON PRESS
© 1978 Overlord Embroidery Pictures
  OVERLORD EMBROIDERY TRUST/
  WHITBREAD & CO LTD
© 1981 Illustration Philip Giggle
This edition first published in 1981 in USA by
Arco Publishing Inc.
219 Park Avenue South
New York, NY 10003

Not for sale in UK, Europe, Commonwealth or
outside USA, Canada, Mexico and Philippines

ISBN: 0 668 05209 0
LCCN 80-28113

Printed and bound in Great Britain

Contents

Acknowledgements

My grateful thanks are extended to all those who have made this a memorable task; to Lord Dulverton, Major-General Douglas Brown and Admiral Sir Charles Madden of the Overlord Embroidery Trust who commissioned the Embroidery and gave my work their blessing. To Messrs Whitbread who gave the facility to publish the book. To Lt-Col W. B. R. Neave-Hill who put me right on a number of points of historical fact. And finally to Ian Morley-Clarke and his production team who seem to have been able to make reasonable sense of my ideas.

Brian Jewell
Tunbridge Wells, 1981

Preface by The Rt. Hon. Lord Dulverton C.B.E.

As commemorative works these two embroideries may depict contrasting sides of English military history, but as a tribute not just to victory and defeat, but to the struggles and sacrifices of war, they stand together. The Overlord Embroidery with, it could be argued, its broader view of war and its effects on not only military but civilian life, nevertheless owes its origins to the Bayeux Tapestry.

Both are a triumph of the imaginative combination of artistic form used to record events of vital significance to the course of English history.

Dulverton.

WESTMINSTER

BOSHAM

WESSEX

ST. VALERY

BAYEUX

ROUEN

MONT ST. MICHEL

RENNES

NORMANDY

CONQUEST

The Bayeux Tapestry

Norman Invasion
October 1066

Foreword

by Joan Edwards

The Bayeux Tapestry tells the story of the invasion of England by William the Conqueror and the defeat of King Harold at the Battle of Hastings. No Englishman can have wished to be reminded of those events, so it is likely that the idea of recording them originated with a Norman. This was probably William's half-brother, Odo, Bishop of Bayeux, who figures on the Tapestry and is known to have liked beautiful and costly furnishings. It may have been commissioned for his palace at Bayeux and later reached the cathedral where, in 1472, it appears in an inventory of its most valuable possessions.

Although displayed annually in the cathedral on the Feast of Relics of St. John, the Tapestry was virtually unknown outside Bayeux until the eighteenth century, when rumours of the existence of a narrative embroidery connected in some way with William the Conqueror began to circulate.

The first publication of representations of the Tapestry was by Bernard de Montfaucon in his *Monuments de la Monarchie Francaise* (1729-33). Through the publication in 1819 of Charles Stothard's famous drawings of the Tapestry, many English people heard of it for the first time. He was dismayed to find the edges torn and that in places the embroidery had completely disappeared. He had, therefore, to reconstruct the pattern from the needle pricks. Not everybody admired it and some declared the design was infantile and the embroidery coarse.

During the French Revolution the Tapestry came near to being cut up to be used as wagon covers but was rescued in 1792 by a local dignitary who stored it through the upheaval.

In 1803 it was exhibited in Paris, where Napoleon, then planning to follow William's example, went to see it, and studied the scene with the mysterious comet closely. It is said that in 1941 Hitler, too, sought an omen or sign in it.

In 1945 a permanent gallery was built in the Bishop's Palace opposite the cathedral, where the Tapestry is exhibited today.

The Bayeux Tapestry was worked by professional embroiderers and not, as many suppose, by Queen Matilda and her ladies. It is 70.4 metres long and 50 centimetres wide. Embroideries on this scale cannot be worked in the hand; neither can two of its principal stitches, couching and laid work. It is reasonably certain, therefore, that the design was transferred to linen and then mounted on an embroidery frame. This would be of sufficient length to enable at least four embroiderers to sit round it at the same time.

Couching and laid work are usually associated with gold embroidery in which as much of the costly metal thread as possible must be left on the front of the work, and little, if any, is taken through to the back. So although in many places the Bayeux Tapestry is covered with stitches, we know the embroiderers used comparatively little wool in proportion to the effect created. The long, fine, calligraphic lines used for outlining, draperies, faces, and other details are in stem and outline stitches.

Because these worsted spun wools called crewels are tough and fairly coarse it is obvious that the embroiderers used strong, large-eyed needles and could cover the ground quite quickly. The eight

---

Chronology

c.1022	Birth of Harold, second son of Earl Godwine.	c.1064	The mysterious adventure of Harold in the territory of Guy of Ponthieu and Normandy, and his part in the military campaign in Britanny.	25 Sep 1066	The English defeat Harald Hardrada and Tostig at the Battle of Stamford Bridge.
c.1027	Birth of William at Falaise.			27 Sep 1066	Norman invasion fleet sails from St. Valery.
1035	William becomes Duke of Normandy.	1065	Tostig ousted as Earl of Northumbria. Harold recognises Moncar, Tostig's successor.	28 Sep 1066	Norman army lands at Pevensey.
c.1036	Birth of Odo, William's half-brother and later Bishop of Bayeux.			2 Oct 1066	Harold marches southward with depleted army.
1042	Coronation of Edward the Confessor.	28 Dec 1065	Edward the Confessor's new abbey church at Westminster consecrated.	14 Oct 1066	Battle of Hastings. Harold slain.
1051	Harold, his father and brothers, banished from England. Harold taking refuge in Ireland. Probable visit to Westminster by William.	5 Jan 1066	Death of Edward the Confessor.	25 Dec 1066	Coronation of William I at Westminster Abbey.
		6 Jan 1066	Funeral of Edward the Confessor. Coronation of Harold II in Westminster Abbey.	1067	Bishop Odo installed as Earl of Kent. Odo commissions the Bayeux Tapestry.
1052	Harold and Godwine return to England.	Apr 1066	Comet (Halley's) seen at its brightest.	c.1067-70	Bayeux Tapestry made in England.
1053	Marriage of William and Matilda, daughter of Baldwin V of Flanders. Death of Godwine, his son Harold succeeding him as Earl of Wessex.	May 1066	Tostig raids the south coast of England.	1077	Dedication of the new cathedral of Bayeux.
		12 Aug 1066	William's invasion fleet is assembled at the mouth of the River Dives.	1082	Bishop Odo loses favour and is imprisoned at Rouen.
1055-7	Conflict between Harold and Aelfgar, Earl of Mercia, who is contesting Harold's growing power.	Sep 1066	The invasion fleet moves to the River Somme, off St. Valery.	1087	Death of William at Mantes. His burial at Caen. Odo released and returns to England.
		Sep 1066	Harald Hardrada, King of Norway, and Tostig bring a large army up the River Humber.	1088	Odo again flees to France.
1063	Harold and his brother Tostig invade Wales and defeat Gruffyd who was an ally of Aelfgar.	20 Sep 1066	Edwin and Moncar's forces defeated at the Battle of Fulford.	1097	Death of Odo in Palermo, Sicily. He is buried in Palermo Cathedral.

colours – buff, pinkish terracotta, yellow, two blues and three greens – were produced from vegetable dyes.

The Tapestry has suffered some rough treatment in its long history and has been restored on more than one occasion. It is generally accepted that it is now incomplete, ending, as it does, abruptly with the pursuit by the Normans after the battle, and not, as may be logically expected, with the Coronation of William in Westminster Abbey.

If, as scholars agree, the embroidery was carried out in several different workrooms (probably situated in Kent), and given the experience and ingenuity of the embroiderers themselves, there is no reason to think it took an excessively long time to make the Bayeux Tapestry. The date now assigned to it is between 1076 and 1086.

Harold as depicted in an early part of the Bayeux Tapestry. Here he is on his way to Bosham at the head of his party and accompanied by hunting dogs. Note the hawk on Harold's wrist and the collars on the dogs with what are believed to be leash rings. Other points of historical interest are the spurs, stirrups and the high-backed saddle with a breast strap. Throughout the Tapestry off-side legs of men and animals are given contrasting colours; the method of giving depth to embroidery. Characters in the margins of the Tapestry seem meaningless in some places whereas in others, such as the battle, they present a highly graphic background.

I. Prelude

Although the Bayeux Tapestry begins in what was probably the year 1064, the events that led to the invasion and conquest of England by William, Duke of Normandy, can be said to have stemmed from the reign of Canute, the Danish King of England who died in 1035. During Canute's reign Edward – known as the Confessor – was banished and accepted asylum in Normandy.

By 1041 in the reign of Hardicanute the climate had sufficiently changed to allow him to return to England, and when Hardicanute died in 1042 Edward became King in his place.

Edward the Confessor naturally felt an affiliation and affection for the Normans not only because of the hospitality he had enjoyed in his years of exile; but because his mother was a daughter of Richard I, Duke of Normandy and sister of the grandfather of William. He freely appointed Normans to high office at his Court and in the Church. This was not to the liking of Godwine, Earl of Wessex, whose ambitious endeavours had gained him a most powerful and influential position.

In 1045 Godwine was able to claim a relationship to the throne when Edward married Edith, Godwine's daughter. This despite the fact that nine years earlier, in 1036, Godwine had been instrumental in the murder of Edward's brother, the Atheling Alfred. In 1051, mainly because of his outspoken criticisms of Edward's Norman favourites, Godwine and his family, including his son Harold, Earl of the East Angles were exiled; Godwine to Flanders and Harold to Ireland, and Edward dismissed his queen, Edith.

However, the disfavour was short-lived and Godwine and his family returned with greater influence than ever in the following year. Exploiting his advantage Godwine demanded and obtained the dismissal of many Normans from their high positions, including that of the Archbishop of Canterbury. Stigand, who had been Chaplain to Canute, replacing Robert of Jumieges as Archbishop. The dismissal of Robert was an action destined to have far reaching consequences as it so angered the Papacy that when, in 1066, Pope Alexander II was petitioned by William, he issued a Bull declaring William the rightful claimant to the throne and Harold a usurper.

In the time of Godwine's and Harold's absence abroad, Edward is said to have received and welcomed William, Duke of Normandy to his Court and it was on this occasion that, according to the Norman chroniclers, Edward made a formal promise to William that he would succeed as King of England.

In 1053 Godwine died and his son Harold succeeded him as Earl of Wessex, and over the next 13 years Harold was able to establish himself as the most powerful noble in England and in such favour with Edward and the Witenagemot or Witan (the King's advisory council made up of nobles, ecclesiastics and officers of the household) that he became recognised as the monarch presumptive in the absence of a direct heir to Edward's crown.

We do not know if William was aware of Harold's standing, or if Harold knew of Edward's alleged promise to William, but what is clear is that Edward's inability to father an heir, or at least to openly nominate his successor, was destined to change the history of England from the time of his death.

PANELS 1 – 4   The landing of Harold and his party in France, probably in the year 1064, is something of a historical mystery. What was he doing there?

The three kings of the period covered by the Bayeux Tapestry portrayed in coins. The first, from about 1053-6 shows Edward the Confessor and is inscribed "AEdvveard Rex". The second, of Harold II, from about 1066 is inscribed "Harold Rex Angl(orum)". The third, from about 1066-68 is of William I, inscribed "Willemus Rex A(nglorum)". Anglo-Saxon coins were mostly silver pennies although gold pennies were minted in small numbers. The penny was derived from the Roman denarius and was the 'd' of the £.s.d. system that survived in Britain until decimilisation. The first pennies were the same weight and size as the denier of Pepin, the father of Charlemagne, king of the Franks. The weight was later increased to 24 grains or one pennyweight. Anglo-Saxon coins were minted in a large number of centres, from Axbridge (Acxepo or Agepor) to York (Eboraci or Eoferpic). The name of the place of minting as well as that of the person responsible for the issue was carried on the coins.

KING EDWARD: WHERE HAROLD DUKE OF THE ENGLISH AND HIS KNIGHTS RIDE

TO BOSHAM: THE CHURCH: HERE HAROLD

SAILED THE SEA   AND WITH THE WIND FULL IN HIS SAILS HE CAME TO THE COUNTRY OF COUNT

3

GUY (OF PONTHIEU): HAROLD: HERE GUY SEIZES HAROLD:

4

The opening scene of the Bayeux Tapestry shows Edward, presumably at Westminster, talking to Harold and, according to the Norman chroniclers, commanding him to reaffirm William as successor to the throne. But this raises the question: why should Edward have chosen Harold as an ambassador? Also, if he were going to visit William, why did Harold land in Ponthieu on the north bank of the Somme – as the Bayeux Tapestry shows us – rather than making for the River Seine and William's capital at Rouen, or some other part of the extensive coast of Normandy.

Many authorities believe that Harold did not go to France intentionally but, when he embarked at Bosham, as the Tapestry shows, the destination was to be either London or some port along the coast; that he was blown by a storm across the Channel to Ponthieu. Furthermore, the presence of a hawk and dogs has been taken by some to suggest Harold was embarking on an intended hunting trip.

Another question that occurs is, if the opening scene shows Harold talking to Edward in Westminster, why does the next sequence show him riding with his men to Bosham near Chichester, and feasting at his manor house instead of embarking direct for Normandy?

Although four ships are shown in the Tapestry, making it look like a small invasion, it is thought that only one vessel was employed.

PANELS 5 – 6   On landing Harold appears to have been taken prisoner by Guy of Ponthieu and held at the castle at Beaurain. Harold is shown holding a sheathed sword while in conversation with Guy – probably a sign that Guy had put him on trust.

PANELS 7 – 8   The Bayeux Tapestry portrays the next event in reverse order. Word reached William of Harold's presence at Beaurain but is not clear who was the bearer of this intelligence – possibly an escaped member of Harold's party. However, it seems likely that Guy, realising the importance of the personage he had as hostage, despatched a courier to William asking advice on the course of action to be taken.

William's response appears to have been prompt and we see his envoys relaying the Duke's instructions that Harold was to be released to him.

PANELS 9 – 10   Guy of Ponthieu escorted Harold to a rendezvous point with William, and the English Earl became the guest of the Norman Duke and was taken to Rouen.

Harold's status at Rouen is not known nor is the degree of amiability between the two contenders for the English throne. The Tapestry suggests a cordial relationship but then this is a Norman commissioned work and would naturally show William in the best possible light, as a generous host. There is even a belief that Harold promised to marry one of William's daughters, although the Englishman was some eight years older than his host.

English Earldoms before the Conquest of 1066.

AND LED HIM TO BEAURAIN AND KEPT HIM THERE:

WHERE HAROLD AND GUY DISCUSS THE MATTER:

UBI·HARO LD·JUUIDO·PARABO LANT· UBI·NUNT

6

WHERE THE MESSENGERS OF DUKE WILLIAM CAME TO GUY: TUROLD:

7

UBI·NUNTII·VVILLELMI· DUCIS·VENERUNT·ADVVIDO NẼ

TUROLD

14

WILLIAM'S MESSENGERS: HERE COMES THE MESSENGER TO DUKE WILLIAM:

8

9

HERE GUY BROUGHT HAROLD TO WILLIAM DUKE OF THE NORMANS:

10

PANEL 11 The Tapestry now poses another mystery in a scene inscribed as 'Where a clerk and Aelfgyva'. This shows an ecclesiastic in conversation with a woman (one of the very few females to appear in the Tapestry). The nature of the topic is not made clear but there is possibly a clue in the lower margin where a naked and lewdly posed man is shown mirroring the same hand gesture as that of the churchman. The fact that this event is depicted with others concerning William and Harold suggests they are connected. Who was Aelfgyva and what part does she play in the plot? It is possible that the designer of the Tapestry is suggesting, in a none too subtle but still oblique manner, that William, as a good host, even provided for the sensual pleasures of his guest.

Aelfgyva is shown in the Tapestry wearing a veil and long-sleeved super-tunic, or *roc*. This is similar attire to the woman leaving the burning house in panel (34). These are the only examples of women's clothing shown in the Tapestry apart from that of Queen Edith at the death of Edward the Confessor in panel (20). Here Edith is shown wearing a long gown and veil.

PANEL 12 According to the chronicler William of Poitiers, the whole of Brittany under Conan had risen in arms against the Normans. For years Conan had been under the guardianship of his uncle, Eudo, but eventually he revolted and made Eudo a prisoner, deciding to take up arms against Normandy.

It was against this background that William led a military expedition into Brittany, inviting Harold to accompany him as a colleague-in-arms.

PANEL 13 Harold is shown in the Tapestry rescuing some of William's men from the quicksands of the River Couesnon, and it seems surprising that the Tapestry shows the English Earl in such a heroic light.

Note the 'kite-shaped' shields, probably of wood covered in leather. It was carried in one of two ways: either from a strap round the neck, or with the left arm through the other two straps. Many shields bore designs for identification in battle.

PANELS 14 – 15 The Normans attacked the town of Dol and Count Conan is shown in the Tapestry as escaping from the castle at Dol by climbing down a rope. The Tapestry is in error for, in fact, Conan was the one laying siege to Dol, which was held for the Normans by a Breton lord. Conan was forced to flee when he heard that William's force was on its way. The curious representation on the left of the castle has been described as a drawbridge, but it is perhaps simply a stylised doorway.

The Normans then pursued Conan through Brittany, via Rennes and finally caught up with him at Dinan, only a short distance from where they started at Dol. At Dinan, Conan and his followers put up a stiff resistance but eventually surrendered.

Duchy of Normandy and neighbours in 1066.

16

TO HIS PALACE: WHERE A CLERK AND AELFGYVA:

11

HERE DUKE WILLIAM AND HIS ARMY CAME TO MONT SAINT MICHEL: AND HERE

12

THEY CROSSED THE RIVER COUESNON: HERE DUKE HAROLD DRAGGED THEM OUT OF THE SAND: AND THEY

13

CAME TO DOL AND CONAN TURNED TO FLIGHT: RENNES: HERE DUKE WILLIAM'S MEN

14

FIGHT AGAINST THE MEN OF DINAN:

15

AND CONAN OFFERED UP THE KEYS: HERE WILLIAM GAVE ARMS TO HAROLD: HERE WILLIAM

16

PANEL 16 The next scene in the Tapestry is described as 'giving him arms', which commonly implies the granting of a knighthood. This cannot be in the case of Harold as he was already an Earl in his own right. Conceivably it was the equivalent to the more modern custom of awarding a medal but most authorities believe it was Harold being made 'William's man', perhaps even forcing him to be a vassal.

It will be seen that William is wearing rank tabs at the back of the neck as marks of identification to those riding behind.

PANEL 17 William and Harold then appear to have travelled to some other place (probably Bayeux, but Bonneville, Bur and Rouen have all been put forward by historians) where Harold undertook some form of oath or act of homage to William. It has been suggested that Harold swore on relics of saints that he would do all in his power to ensure that William succeeded to the English throne. If this is true, then it must be presumed that the oath was made under duress. It was this oath-taking that was later to lead to the Pope's condemnation of perjury and blasphemy.

The Tapestry here and in other places clearly shows the costume of the period: the above or below the knee tunic, worn with a girdle. Sleeves were close-fitting, and the skirt of the tunic was often slit at the front and rear so that the two parts could be wrapped round the legs and taped for riding on horseback. Most men of higher rank are shown with cloaks, open at the front and secured in place with a brooch. The legs seem to be covered with stockings and sometimes leg bandages. These may have been tights or covers for breeches. Headgear, other than helmets, is almost completely absent in the Tapestry, apart from *Phrygian* bonnets which appear in a few places.

PANELS 18–19 William, having gained what he needed from Harold in the form of sworn allegiance, no longer needed him and Harold was free to return to England, ending what seems to have been a most unfortunate encounter with his adversary.

Back at Westminster, Harold was given audience by Edward the Confessor, who is shown looking drawn and feeble. It has been suggested this was part of the Norman propaganda purpose of the Tapestry, as the king was to remain quite healthy for a further eighteen months or so.

Edward receiving Harold returning from Normandy. Edward is shown aged and ill – Norman propaganda to justify the invasion.

Saxon Homelife

The church of St. Mary the Virgin at Sompting. It was rebuilt in the twelfth century by a Knights Templar, who attached a chapel to the south side. The site was originally a Saxon church, of which only the tower remains. The tower is about 19 feet square in plan, and has no buttresses; the strengthening being by corner pilasters of long and short rectangular stones. It has the only British example of a 'Rheinish helm' spire.

An English house at the time of the Norman invasion. These were traditionally built with a wooden floor covering a pit. Recent research has suggested that the pit provided a damp course; the floor was supported over it to keep the floorboards well away from the damp ground.
Inside the reconstructed family house the prominent feature is the round clay hearth for the fire. The thatched roof is supported by hazel hurdling.

Two panels from an illuminated eleventh century Saxon calendar, showing the months of October and August. The October panel is of a hunting scene with falcons. These were introduced to England in the ninth century and were a popular sport with the nobility. The August scene shows peasants reaping their lord's estates with scythes and pitchforks before tending to their own land.

A fine gold, enamel and ivory cross made in Edward the Confessor's reign, originally containing a relic.

The Bayeux Tapestry

CAME TO BAYEUX: WHERE HAROLD MADE AN OATH TO DUKE WILLIAM: HERE DUKE

17

18 HAROLD RETURNED TO ENGLISH SOIL:

22

AND CAME TO KING EDWARD   HERE IS THE BODY OF KING EDWARD CARRIED

19

II. Harold's Reign

PANEL 20   In December 1065, Edward the Confessor, after having reigned since 1042, was suddenly taken ill and died on the 5 January. Although losing the power of speech, Edward is said to have awoke before he died and, in the presence of the Queen, Stigand the Archbishop of Canterbury and Robert the Staler, probably Master of the King's stables, pointed to Harold and said 'I commend my wife to your care and with her my whole kingdom'.

Immediately below Edward's death scene, the King is being laid out for burial. Again the Tapestry shows scenes in reverse order, with Edward's funeral procession before his death. The funeral procession was led by Abbot Eadwine of Westminster, who is seen in the Tapestry carrying a crosier. Note the almost modern looking prayer books.

The fact that the Abbey is newly completed is symbolised in the Tapestry by a workman fixing a weather cock.

PANEL 21   The Witan met immediately after Edward's death and elected Harold as King. Note

Harold holding the formidable Danish battleaxe. The other axe being offered, together with the crown, was the official symbol of authority.

The coronation took place in the new Westminster Abbey, the rebuilt church of St. Peter on Thorney Island, on the following day – the same day as Edward's remains were interred.

Although the Witan were unanimous in their support of Harold as king, the population of Northumbria, being mainly Danish, found the election unacceptable, contending that their own Moncar, Earl of Mercia, or his brother Edwin, had equally strong claims to the throne of England.

Towards the end of January Harold rode to York and with the aid of Wulfstan, the Bishop of Worcester, was able to win over the Northumbrian leaders.

In February, as a means of strengthening ties between north and south, Harold married Ealdgy, or Edith, sister of Moncar and Edwin and, incidentally, widow of Prince Gruffyd of Wales, who had met his death during Harold's campaigns against the Welsh.

PANEL 22   In the spring of 1066 the comet, we now know as Halley's Comet, but then called 'the hairy

star', blazed across the night sky, prompting superstitious speculation as to whether it was a good or bad omen. It seems that it may have caused more of a stir in England than in Normandy as the Bayeux Tapestry shows the comet and its spectators in the same section where Harold is depicted. Note the suggestion of an invasion fleet in the margin below Harold's palace.

PANEL 23   The news of Edward's death and the crowning of Harold was told to William probably while hunting at Quevilly. Immediately the Duke returned to Rouen and after sending an ultimatum to Harold, which was rejected, he decided upon the invasion of England.

In February, William held a council of Norman barons at Lillebonne, announcing his intention of taking the English crown by force, persuading those with doubts on the justification for such action with promises of land and rewards. The council included William's half-brother Odo, Bishop of Bayeux, a key figure throughout the Tapestry and who commissioned this work of art after the Conquest.

Harold's brother, Tostig, exiled in Flanders, was one of those who assured William of support. Tostig

TO THE CHURCH OF
ST. PETER THE APOSTLE

HERE KING EDWARD IN BED HARANGUES HIS FAITHFUL FRIENDS:
AND HERE IS HE DEAD:

20

HERE THEY HAVE GIVEN THE
KING'S CROWN TO HAROLD:

HERE SITS HAROLD THE
KING OF THE ENGLISH:

STIGAND THE
ARCHBISHOP:

21

24

had been made Earl of Northumbria in 1055 but, because of his strict rule, the people had risen in 1065 and deposed him, choosing Moncar in his place. Tostig was doubtful that William, to whom he was related by marriage, would help in his aims against his brother, and began to assemble his own hired ships and men for independent action.

PANEL 24 Building of the Norman invasion fleet began in March. The ships were based on the Viking vessels of the 9th century. Their measurements varied between 80 and 140 feet long and 16 to 28 feet in width and needed up to 30 oarsmen on each side for propulsion apart from the single square sail. Directional control was by steering oar pivoted on the right quarter.

The Tapestry shows the ships very much reduced in size – an unavoidable misrepresentation. There is, however, a more serious distortion in the Tapestry; that of displaying the shields along the gunwales, where they would interfere with the movement of the oars. Shields were only placed along the gunwales when the ship was at anchor or in port and then on the outside and not the inside as is sometimes depicted in the Tapestry.

At about the same time as the building of the fleet started, William despatched emmisaries to most European kings and barons, calling for their support or at least their neutrality in the forthcoming military adventure. One who gave his whole-hearted support to William's cause was Eustace, Count of Boulogne, who had been insulted by Harold's father, Godwine, as far back as 1051.

What the Bayeux Tapestry does not show is the activity in England during the spring and summer of 1066. Well aware of William's invasion plans, Harold prepared to defend his crown by mobilising his forces.

PANEL 25 In May, Pope Alexander II gave his blessing to Duke William's cause, issuing a Bull condemning Harold as a usurper. As tokens of papal support, William was sent a ring containing 'a hair of St. Peter' and a consecrated banner that was carried by the Normans in the invasion and at the Battle of

A moment that changed the course of British history. On 6 January 1066 the leading nobles of the Witan – more an advisory council than a parliament – offered the crown of England to Harold. An obvious choice considering Harold's prominence in the country, but a decision that was to make the Norman invasion inevitable.

THESE MEN MARVEL AT THE STAR: HAROLD: HERE AN ENGLISH SHIP CAME

22

TO THE LAND OF DUKE WILLIAM   HERE DUKE WILLIAM ORDERED THEM TO BUILD

23

24

HERE THE SHIPS ARE DRAGGED TO THE SEA:

25

Hastings. Thus William's campaign was considered a Holy crusade.

Harold's estranged brother, Tostig, sailed his hired fleet to the Isle of Wight where he demanded money and provisions. From here the fleet worked its way along the Sussex and Kent coasts, burning and pillaging as it went. At Sandwich, Harold attempted to intercept his brother but his force arrived too late and Tostig sailed north to the Humber and raided the coast of Lindsey, an action that caused the Earls Moncar and Edwin to partially mobilise the northern Fyrd (see page 32). Tostig sailed for Scotland, taking refuge for several months with King Malcolm III.

Still bitterly desperate to avenge himself on his brother, Tostig began negotiations with Harald Hardrada, King of Norway. Harald Hardrada considered that he also had a claim to the English throne based on a pact made between his father and King Hardicanute.

Harald Hardrada's army and fleet began assembling in July, augmented by contingents from Scotland, Ireland, the Orkney and Shetland islands and Iceland.

In England, King Harold called out the Fyrd in the southern shires; London and the Cinque Ports were commanded to furnish a fleet of ships to defend the south coast. Mobilisation at this time was, with hindsight, a major error as the invasion was not imminent, and the statutory period that the Fyrd was required to serve was only two months. This period would therefore end, even for the last to be called up in this emergency, on 8 September. However, Harold's decision to muster his defences at such an early date was perhaps prompted by the aggression of his brother Tostig. Harold made the Isle of Wight his defensive headquarters and from there directed the army and fleet.

It is remarkable how William was able to muster sufficient skilled labour to build the invasion fleet. Shipwrights must have been brought in from other lands and 'crash courses' given to unskilled workers from his own country, in order to produce the quantity and quality of workmanship at the necessary speed. Although, by necessity, the ships are shown in a fore-shortened form in the Tapestry, they were in fact between 80 and 140 feet long and from 16 to 28 feet wide, not unlike the Viking longboats that had ruled the seas over the previous centuries. The workmen in the Tapestry appear to be using what could be a hammer and an axe, while the man in the background may be using a form of drill.

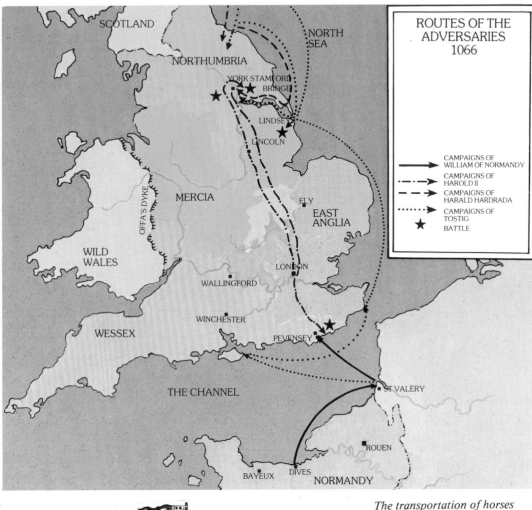

ROUTES OF THE
ADVERSARIES
1066

CAMPAIGNS OF
WILLIAM OF NORMANDY

CAMPAIGNS OF
HAROLD II

CAMPAIGNS OF
HARALD HARDRADA

CAMPAIGNS OF
TOSTIG

★ BATTLE

PANEL 26 The number of ships in the fleet is not known but a Norman chronicler was to write later:

'. . . I heard my father say, and this I remember well, although I was a lad at the time, that, when they set sail from Saint-Valery [see page 35], counting boats, smaller vessels and skiffs carrying arms and armour, the fleet was 696 strong. I have read, and whether this is true or not I cannot say, that there were as many as 3000 vessels with their sails and masts'.

They had been built in harbours and rivers along the Normandy coast and, by July, began to assemble at the mouth of the River Dives, a short distance north east of Caen and where the 6th British Airborne Division was to land some 900 years later.

It is thought each of William's invasion ships had a capacity of nine men and horses or 25 men only.

PANELS 27 – 29 By 12 August the Normans' invasion preparations had been completed, and William joined his fleet aboard his command ship *Mora* and waited nearly a month for a suitable southerly wind. The administration of affairs in Normandy was entrusted to William's wife, Matilda, and Roger of Beaumont.

The other invasion fleet, that of Harald Hardrada, had been assembled near Bergen, and in August, set sail to be joined at Orkney by the fleets of Tostig and the other contingents. According to one chronicler there were in Harald Hardrada's fleet some 200 fighting ships, not counting supply ships and small craft.

King Harold's militia army had now been mobilised for four months and the King was by now facing demands for its disbandment: provisions were running

to page 35

The routes of the combatant forces in 1066: Tostig's campaign from May, Harald Hardrada's enterprise, Harold's route of march, and William's crossing.

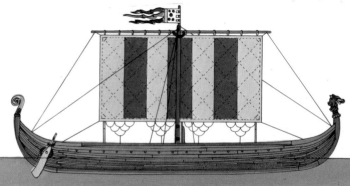

The transportation of horses in the Norman invasion fleet could not have been easy, but imperative, as the cavalry's role in the invasion was a vital one. The problem was presumably overcome before the invasion and probably involved the design of the boats, enabling the sideways loading and unloading of the living cargoes. Once on board, the horses would be felled onto their sides and tethered.

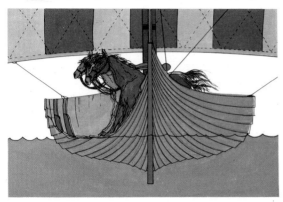

THESE MEN ARE CARRYING ARMS TO THE SHIPS

AND HERE THEY ARE DRAGGING A CART
LADEN WITH WINE AND ARMS:

26

HERE DUKE WILLIAM IN A GREAT SHIP

27

CROSSED THE SEA

MAR E TRAN SIVIT ETVENIT

28

AND CAME TO PEVENSEY:

29

AD PEVENE SÆ:· HIC EXEVNT:CABA

HERE ARE THE HORSES
LEAVING THE BOATS:

AND HERE THE SOLDIERS HAVE HASTENED TO HASTINGS

30

*To land the horses, ships were probably beached broadside to the shore and
the horses cut loose to roll the ship sideways so that they could jump off into
shallow water.*

34

from page 29

short and if the men did not return to the land the harvest would rot in the fields, resulting in winter famine. On 8 September it was agreed that the shire levies of the Fyrd could return to their homes and the defence fleet was ordered to London to disband. However, in the north the Earls Moncar and Edwin mustered the northern Fyrd on news of the sailing of Harald Hardrada's fleets.

On 12 September William's fleet moved to St. Valery and replenished provisions. At this time a storm blew up in the Channel and some of William's ships were lost. For the English fleet on its way to London, the storm was disastrous – most of the ships being sunk or scattered.

Harald Hardrada's force began ravaging the coast from the Tees to the Est, attacking Scarborough and Holderness, and finally sailed up the Humber and Ouse as far as Riccall, and immediately marched on York. On hearing this Harold, now in Westminster, set off to the north with his housecarls. Before he could reach Yorkshire, the invaders met the English led by Moncar and Edwin at Fulford Gate on 20 September and routed them. York surrendered four

days later and Harald Hardrada set up his camp at Stamford Bridge on the River Derwent.

On 25 September Harold, after his forced march, took the invaders by surprise and was victorious, but not without heavy losses. In the battle both Harald Hardrada and Tostig fell victims to the English swords. We assume on his march to the north, Harold mobilised the Fyrd who joined him along the road.

On the night of 27 September, William's fleet sailed from St Valery in the Somme estuary under an easterly wind headed by William's ship *Mora*, which had been presented to him by his wife Matilda.

The crossing is described by the Norman chronicler, William of Poitiers: 'In the night a trumpet sounded from *Mora* and at this signal the fleet weighed anchor and put to sea. The *Mora* being the faster of the ships, was ahead of the fleet when dawn broke. To allow the slower vessels to catch up, the *Mora* dropped anchor . . .'

PANEL 30   William's fleet made landfall at Pevensey on the morning of 28 September. This is described by William of Poitiers:

Having been carried to Pevensey by a prosperous wind he disembarked without opposition . . . William quickly explored the places, and the inhabitants,

himself, accompanied by a band of not more than 25 soldiers . . . returning from this on foot on account o the roughness of the bye-paths.

PANELS 31 – 33   On 29 September William set up his headquarters at Hastings and his men began foraging for food and pillaging in the surrounding area with the aim of enticing Harold to action.

The scene in the Tapestry showing the preparation of food is interesting, representing in some detail how the higher command fared during a campaign. First there is the killing of the animals, and in this scene the Tapestry specifically mentions a knight by the name of Wadard, who was possibly in charge of foraging; Wadard's name was later to appear in the Domesday Book as holding lands in England under Bishop Odo. We see the boiling of the meat in a hanging pot, fowls on spits and bread being baked. The cooks are then passing the food to the waiting servants who place it on a table formed from shields laid on trestles. A 'mess call' is being blown on a horn. At the table Bishop Odo blesses the food.

PANELS 33, 34   The next scene shows William holding a conference in a tiled-roof building with Bishop Odo

TO SEIZE FOOD: HERE IS WADARD:

31

HERE IS THE MEAT
BEING COOKED,

AND HERE THE SERVANTS
HAVE SERVED IT UP:

HERE THEY MADE A BANQUET,

32

AND HERE THE BISHOP BLESSES
THE FOOD AND DRINK:

BISHOP ODO,
WILLIAM, ROBERT:

THIS MAN HAD COMMANDED THAT A CASTLE

33

SHOULD BE THROWN UP
AT HASTINGS:

HERE NEWS IS BROUGHT TO
WILLIAM ABOUT HAROLD:

HERE A HOUSE
IS BURNED:

and Robert of Mortain, his two half-brothers.

The Tapestry shows the building of fortifications. Two of the working men seem to be engaged in a bout with cudgels which may have been an expression of boisterous recreation, or it could have been an example of coercing Englishmen into a labour force.

William's choice of Hastings as a base rather than Pevensey was almost certainly through practical necessity. Pevensey in those days was on a peninsular of marshland; not only was it an inhospitable site for a base but any progress inland would be near impossible. However, before taking his ships to Hastings, William did establish a garrison at Pevensey within the old Roman fort there.

In the same panel there is depicted a house being burned at Hastings with a well dressed woman leading a small boy away by the hand. This incident has been the subject of speculation among historians. Was her house being burned by the Normans in order to draw Harold's attack? Or was it, as had been suggested, an act of reprisal by the English community against someone who has been collaborating with the enemy? We shall never know.

The intelligence systems of the two armies is worthy of note. The Tapestry shows news of Harold's movements being told to William, by one, Robert, son of Guimara, a Norman living in England. It took five days for news of the Normans landing to reach Harold in York – 260 miles away, although it is thought by some historians that he had already started on the road back to London when the messenger met him. Once again, he had to march against an invader, taking with him his housecarls, leaving much of the Fyrd with Moncar and Edwin.

On the march from York to London shire levies were gathered, and once back at the capital Harold issued orders for the remobilisation of the Fyrd of the southern shires.

William sent the Monk of Fecamp as a courier to Harold proposing that their rival claims should be submitted to law. But Harold spurned the suggestion and marched out of London on 11 or 12 October. On 13 October Harold formed up his army on a hill on which the town of Battle now stands. This venue selected by the English King was undoubtedly influenced by the availability of suitable roads.

The next morning the Normans attacked and so began the most important battle to be fought on English soil, changing, as it did, the course of the nation's history.

III. The Battle

We have to accept that the Battle of Hastings as depicted in the Bayeux Tapestry is a stylised portrayal of events that did not occur in the sequence as shown.

Military historians have, over the years, pieced together logical tactical situations and, together with the accounts of the chroniclers, have been able to reconstruct a likely chain of events. The battle almost certainly was divided into four definite phases:
1. Attack by the Norman archers, which had no effect.
2. Advance and attack by Norman men-at-arms, which was repulsed.
3. Charge by Norman cavalry, again unsuccessful, but was instrumental in cutting off and annihilating a large number of Saxons.
4. Combined attack by cavalry and men-at-arms under covering bombardment by archers. This succeeded in a breakthrough of the Saxon line.

It is excusable to wonder why Harold chose to meet the invaders where he did. It would seem to be a sounder strategy, particularly after the strength-sapping battle at Stamford Bridge and the associated marches at a rate of some 40 miles a day, to have drawn William inland for a decisive battle nearer London. Alternatively, to have waited for his reinforcements from the north and then to have marched on William with a numerically superior force.

A clue to the answer as to why Harold chose this course of action is to be found in his past career as a military commander. Both his major battles – at Rhuddlan in 1063 against Gruffyth ap Llewelyn and against Harald Hardrada at Stamford Bridge, owed their success to surprise, and it presumably seemed reasonable for him to suppose that a similar strategy would work for a third time.

Harold's choice of camp site was based on sound judgment if we are to accept his reason for not tempting William inland towards London. The invader would have to pass this way en route to London, it made an excellent defensive stronghold for foot soldiers against cavalry and archers, and it was within a short distance of Hastings and William's camp so that a surprise attack could be made once the English forces had been consolidated. Harold would have been familiar with the terrain being lord of several nearby manors and having visited the area when preparing the coastal defences.

The scene of the battle, like that of Naseby, is a watershed. The 350 feet high Caldbec Hill, now occupied by Battle High Street, runs southwards flanked on both sides by falling ground. It is part of a complex watershed system that flows into Rye Bay and into the sea at Bulverhythe. The contours of the land are remarkable and worth studying on the map, as the natural features were to make a considerable contribution to the course of the battle.

The greater part of the English force must have arrived on the evening of 13 October, assembling at the landmark called the 'Hoar Apple Tree', on the high ground, the Fyrd coming in from all directions. We can speculate that English forces were arriving through the night and throughout the next day when the battle was in progress.

Harold probably set up his troops in line with Housecarls to the front and backed up by some ten ranks of militia men. Further Housecarls surrounded his command position where flew his two standards: the Dragon of Wessex and the Fighting Man.

PANEL 35, 36 The advance posts of the Norman assembly around Hastings were probably situated on Baldslow Ridge some five miles from Senlac. It is hard

for us now to imagine that armed forces at that time did not form up in concentrations except when engaged in battle. The reason for this dispersement was that armies had to live off the land and a given area could only support a certain number of men. With the foraging went the devastation of numerous villages and an idea of the size of the area occupied by William's army can be gained from the devastated or partly devastated places mentioned in the Domesday Book: Ashburnham, Catsfield, Crowhurst, Guestling, Herstmonceux, Hooe, Mountfield, Netherfield, Salehurst, Sedlescombe and Whatlington, among others that are now impossible to identify successfully.

News of Harold's approach reached William on the 13 October and his decision to attack would have been made that night. By 0600 hours the next morning the vanguard of the Norman column would have been on the move.

The semi-circular war-flag or gonfanon carried on one of the knight's lances in the Tapestry was probably a development of the Norse raven flag.

At about 0700 hours the column, with William at the head, arrived at Telham Hill (Hechelande or Heathland as it was called in 1066).

HERE THE SOLDIERS WENT OUT OF HASTINGS

35

AND CAME TO THE BATTLE AGAINST KING HAROLD:

36

HERE DUKE WILLIAM ASKS VITAL WHETHER HE HAS SEEN HAROLD'S ARMY:

37

PANELS 37 – 39   At Telham Hill William was met by his scout Vital, a vassal of Bishop Odo, who had gone on ahead to reconnoitre. William was informed that Harold's army was formed up at Senlac. Note that William is carrying a mace, a more usual weapon than the sword or lance for a nobleman of high rank and for clerics on the field of battle. Harold was given news of William's approaching column at about the same time. It would seem that both armies were using efficient reconnaissance scouts.

Harold's army appears for the first time in the Bayeux Tapestry with the king receiving news of the Normans' coming to the battleground. Harold is seen mounted and carrying a lance.

PANEL 40   On learning the precise disposition of the English, William halted his column and ordered armour to be worn. The Bayeux Tapestry shows William exhorting his knights to 'prepare manfully', and this in the past has led to the story that he made a speech to his entire army. However, this was impossible as the column would have been at least three miles long.

The formation commanders having been briefed, the column resumed its march, the head reaching the point where the Norman lines would be deployed immediately in front of the English. The deployment involved the placing of the various divisions of William's forces. To the right was the Franco-Flemish Division – men of Boulonnais and the Ile-de-France, under the command of Roger of Montgomerie, Eustace the Count of Boulogne and William FitzOsbern. In the centre, William lined up his own Norman Division with his two half-brothers, Robert, Count of Mortain and Bishop Odo of Bayeux as his subordinates. To the left there was the Breton Division comprising Bretons, Poitevins and Manceaux under the command of Alan Fergant, the Count of Brittany.

The only chronicler to consider the Norman deployment was Wace, who in some respects has proved to be unreliable. However, his description in this regard is convincing. He describes the first column marching cross the valley while the second wheeled and marched to the other end of the line. The Normans then occupied the gap between the other two divisions. A deployment operation of this kind takes some time and one may wonder why the English did not attack before it was completed. There was etiquette of warfare in those times and it was unthinkable to begin fighting before the formations had taken up their positions for a set battle.

William himself established his command post on a hill directly in front of that of Harold.

The lining up of the Normans was uniform throughout the three divisions: archers to the front, backed by men-at-arms with the knights and their followers behind.

PANELS 41, 42   It would have been about 0900 hours on the 14 October before the Norman forces were deployed. Trumpets then sounded and England's most fateful battle had begun.

Notwithstanding the etiquette of battle, it seems remarkable that Harold, whose philosophy in generalship was one of surprise, should have allowed the initiative to pass to the enemy and we can only presume that he considered his position strong enough to withstand any Norman attack and that he planned to counter-attack when the enemy momentum had been spent.

More obvious is William's strategy. From the order in which he placed his classes of soldiers we can see that his intention was to open the attack with his archers, to follow this with a charge of the men-at-arms and then to invade breaches in the English lines with his cavalry.

THIS MAN GIVES NEWS TO KING HAROLD ABOUT DUKE WILLIAM'S ARMY:

HERE DUKE WILLIAM EXHORTS HIS SOLDIERS

39

THAT THEY PREPARE THEMSELVES MANFULLY AND WISELY

40

FOR THE BATTLE AGAINST THE ENGLISH ARMY:

41

42

HERE FELL LEOFWYN AND GYRTH THE BROTHERS OF KING HAROLD:

43

HERE ENGLISH AND FRENCH FELL TOGETHER IN BATTLE:

44

The first stage of this plan opened with the archers advancing to 100 yards of the English lines and shooting their first flight of arrows. (Note the short or Danish bow used by Norman archers). This was not an entirely satisfactory operation as, having to shoot uphill, many of the high arrows passed overhead while those aimed low were held on the shields of the Housecarls in their forward position. (Note the overlapping 'shield-wall' in the Tapestry). Another factor to reduce the effectiveness of the Norman archers was the absence of their English counterparts. It was the practice to rely on the arrows shot by the enemy to replenish supplies and when none were returned by the defenders the Duke's men had to await the arrival of their supply train before shooting further volleys.

Despite the limited effect of the archers, William persisted with his plan and sent in the infantry only to meet the impregnable wall of Housecarls who wrought fearful havoc with their battleaxes. The Bretons, in particular, suffered terribly and broke in disorder to be pursued by some of the Fyrd; against orders – it is said. This disorganised mêlée was swept into the marshy land of the valley where there was great bloodshed.

PANELS 43, 44 Harold's two brothers, Earl Gyrth and Earl Leofwine, were both killed during one of the Norman surges, but it is by no means clear at which stage of the battle this took place. The Tapestry shows it happening before the episode when William lifted his helmet to restore morale, whereas chroniclers reverse this order of events.

PANELS 45, 46 At one stage of the battle the Norman Division, finding they were unsupported on their left by the failing and depleted Bretons, began to fall back. This movement spread along the entire line including the Franco-Flemish Division on the right flank. In his command post William could see that a very dangerous situation was developing. Galloping to where the line seemed in danger of collapse, his horse, a charger that is said to have been presented to him by

The battle would have been a horrific spectacle. Apart from the limited use of bows and arrows, all combat was at close quarters with battleaxes, sword and spear. Victors would have been as bloody as vanquished and such would be the confusion that friend would slay friend. Apart from the barbaric reality, there would have been the sheer exhaustion, with any let up resulting in certain death.

the Spanish king, was killed under him. Soon a rumour was spreading among the Normans that their Duke was dead. Gaining another horse from one of his knights, William rode on into the mêlée lifting his helmet to show he was still alive. With the help of Bishop Odo and Count Eustace of Boulogne, William was able to restore morale and stem the panic.

Detaching some of his cavalry, William ordered them to charge downhill to the marshy land where the English were murderously punishing the Bretons. Unprepared for this cavalry attack, the English were annihilated. In the words of William of Poitiers, 'The eager Normans, outflanking several thousands that had followed them, annihilated them in a moment, so that not even one survived'.

In the Tapestry, Count Eustace is shown carrying what is believed to be the Papal banner. It appeared once previously in the Tapestry; in the scene when news was brought to William at Hastings.

PANEL 47 Sometime during the day it must have been necessary for both sides to withdraw to their lines and reform. This period of reorganisation is not shown in the Bayeux Tapestry, nor is it mentioned by any of the chroniclers. Nevertheless, it is inconceivable that after such a long and bitter struggle, with forces displaced all over the field, it would have been possible for William to have committed his troops to the next stage without a pause.

We may wonder why Harold did not take advantage of this pause to launch a counter-attack and must conclude that his force was so weakened or exhausted that the English also needed time for reorganisation.

William had tried both his archers and infantry in the earlier stages of the battle and had failed to break the English line. He had been forced to use his cavalry when the intention had been to keep them back for the final thrust and pursuit. Having used them thus, he now came to the decision to commit them to the full and issued orders for a general attack.

As the knights assailed the hill they were met by the same murderous resistance that had been earlier experienced by the foot soldiers. It must have been a

Horses have, until recent times, been the innocent victims of warfare. Slain and maimed in agony, the beasts laid a carpet of flesh on battlefields. Remounts would be used when horses were too weary to be ridden. Duke William's horse is said to have been a gift from the Spanish king; when killed under him he is said to have commandeered another mount from one of his knights.

HERE BISHOP ODO HOLDING
A MACE CHEERS ON THE YOUNG MEN:

45

HERE IS DUKE WILLIAM: EUSTACE (OF BOLOUGNE):   HERE ARE THE FRENCH FIGHTING

46

AND THOSE WHO WERE WITH HAROLD HAVE FALLEN:

47

HERE KING HAROLD HAS BEEN KILLED:

48

long and frightful slog with Housecarls' battleaxes eventually proving too much for the Norman Division in the centre. As they fell back so they were pursued by the English Fyrd. Whether or not this was a counter-attack under Harold's orders, we shall never know but it proved to be the beginning of the end for the English. William was able to reform his cavalry and charge down on the Fyrd who had broken ranks effecting massive casualties. Similar chains of events on the right flank involving the Franco-Flemish Division also considerably weakened the English and it became necessary for them to shorten and concentrate their line, but still it remained unbroken. William who, earlier, had used his archers, infantry and cavalry in independent actions, now came to the radical decision of bringing to bear all three components of his army; the archers shooting high, so that their arrows fell from the sky, giving cover to the mixed cavalry and infantry charging up the hill. The Norman archers must, by this time, have been able to replenish their arrows from a supply train at the rear as few, if any, had been returned by the English.

It was at this stage of the battle that Harold is said to have sustained a wound in his eye. There was, and to some extent, still exists, a popular misconception that Harold was killed by an arrow in his eye. Neither the Tapestry or the chroniclers support this legend.

PANEL 48 At last, at about 1500 hours in the afternoon, the Norman cavalry succeeded in gaining the top of the ridge and were able to roll up parts of the thinning English line. From the east a detachment of Franco-Flemish cavalry was performing a similar manoeuvre, under the command of Eustace of Boulogne.

The strong-point of Harold's command post was now being attacked from both flanks, and at last their numbers had so diminished that a small company of Norman knights, named as Guy of Ponthieu, Giffard, Montford and Eustace according to an account by Guy of Amiens, were able to break through and cut down the king at the fateful spot today marked by the 'Norman Stone'. Harold had fought heroically throughout the day. Wrote William of Malmesbury, 'Harold hit out repeatedly at every enemy who came within striking distance, dashing horse and horseman to the ground with a single blow, so that none came near him without paying dearly for it'.

The actual mortal attack on Harold is graphically described by Guy of Amiens: 'With the point of his lance the first pierced Harold's shield and then penetrated his chest, drenching the ground with his blood which poured out in torrents. With his sword the second cut off his head, just below where his helmet protected him. The third disembowelled him with his javelin. The fourth hacked off his leg at the thigh and hurled it far away. Struck down in this way, his dead body lay on the ground'.

PANEL 49 On the death of Harold, the Shire Levies of the Fyrd fled the field of battle but what remained of the Housecarls continued to fight as a rearguard action in the darkening afternoon.

By about 1700 hours the Normans were in complete possession of Senlac Ridge and William ordered an immediate pursuit disregarding the fatigue of his own men. According to William of Poitiers, the English were 'off in all directions, some on horseback, some on foot, some taking to the roads, most by by-paths'.

The pursuit seems to have been led by Eustace of Boulogne, one of Harold's slayers, whose name constantly recurs throughout accounts of the battle,

49

ET FVGA VE R TERVNT ANGLI

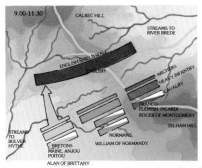

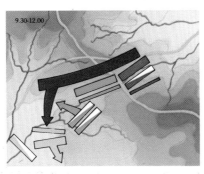

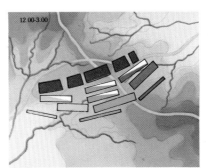

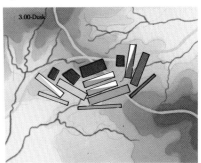

Unsuccessful attack on English Shield Wall. No arrows were returned to replenish supplies.

The Bretons retreated but the Norman cavalry charged and some of the Fyrd were cut off and killed.

The English lines were broken into small sections after six hours of continuous attack.

A concerted attack by archers enabled the cavalry to move in, isolating groups and winning the day.

and was obviously one of William's Chief-of-staff officers. With his pursuing cavalry they encountered a group of Housecarls on a high bank and, unable to judge their number in the growing darkness, Eustace was under the impression that some further English reinforcements had arrived and prudently turned back. He was met by William who sternly reminded him of the order to pursue. At that moment a Housecarl, who apparently had concealed himself at the time of the English rout, crept up and struck Eustace down, although not killing him. William then ordered the pocket of resistance to be eliminated. Which it was, but not without further casualties to the Normans.

Thus, with the pursuit, we come to the end of what survives of the Bayeux Tapestry. There must have been more for it is not the end of the story, even of the day.

IV. The Mystery of the Malfosse

Chroniclers mention the *Malfosse* which may refer to the last stand of Housecarls but there is a certain element of mystery in the accounts, clouding both what happened and the locality, or even if they are concerned with the same incident. It is worthwhile to record these various accounts.

In about 1070, William of Poitiers wrote:

At last the fugitives regained confidence to renew the fight [there is then a confusing reference to a ravine or steep bank and frequent ditches] *But the leader of the victorious hosts, seeing the companies collected thus unexpectedly . . . bade . . . Count Eustace, who was turning away with 50 horsemen, did not depart. The Duke . . . advanced and crushed his opponents. In this action several noble Normans fell, their courage being hampered by the precipitous character of the country'.*

Sometime between 1070 and 1090, William of Jumieges wrote:

The long grass hid from the Normans an ancient bank [this could also be interpreted as a mud wall or causeway] *where the Normans were suddenly thrown from their horses, killing one another as they fell suddenly and without warning, one on the top of the other'.*

Orderic Vital wrote, in about 1125:

But the growing grass hid an ancient bank [mud wall or causeway] *where the galloping Normans with their horses and arms fell down in large numbers; and this, as one after another unexpectedly fell, destroyed them in turn. That, without doubt gave the fleeing English a renewal of confidence. Perceiving the opportunity given by a steep bank and many ditches, they suddenly halted, rallied, and bravely inflicted a great slaughter on the Normans.*

It is generally held that this, or some, if more than one incident, occurred in the area between Caldbec Hill and Oak Wood to the north which contains a stretch of ground referred to in ancient documents as Manfosse – possibly a corruption of Malfosse. But we cannot be certain that this was the place of the Norman post-victory disaster. It is another mystery to add to the others contained in the Bayeux Tapestry, including such lesser teasers as: What was the story behind Aelfgyva and the priest? (see panel 11) and is the man in the last panel really wrestling with snakes?

V. Epilogue

On the day after the battle, Sunday 15 October, may have come the task of burying the dead although there are no chronicled accounts of such burial. It is possible that the corpses were left where they lay. There had been no burial at Stamford Bridge; as witnessed by Orderic Vital writing some 70 years later: 'The site of the battle is obvious to all who travel in those parts. To this day a great congeries of skeletons of those who died still lies there, as evidence of the wholesale slaughter of two peoples.'.

Certainly no cemetery pits have been found at La Place de Battell, or Battle as it has been known since the 19th century. The bodies of Harold, Gyrth and Leofwine were later identified. Their mother Gytha pleaded for Harold's body but was refused by William, and instead, by his command it was buried by the sea.

William, Duke of Normandy and Conqueror of England did not immediately proceed to London but returned with his army to Hastings for a period of recuperation and to await reinforcements from across the Channel.

There can be little doubt that the Bayeux Tapestry originally extended to cover the days after the battle, and the lost section probably culminated with the coronation of William in Westminster Abbey on Christmas Day in 1066.

It could be argued that the Norman Conquest was incomplete, even after William's Coronation, and that England was only his when Hereward the Wake made peace in 1071. In that year Ely, the last refuge of the English defenders was taken, and England was truly conquered.

OVERLORD

The Overlord Embroidery

Normandy Landings
June 1944

Chronology

6 Mar 1944	Daylight raids on Berlin begun by US Eighth Air Force.
2 Apr 1944	Russians enter Roumania.
4 Jun 1944	Fifth Army enters Rome.
6 Jun 1944	D DAY LANDINGS IN NORMANDY.
10 Jun 1944	Russian offensive against Finland.
13 Jun 1944	First V1 Flying Bomb drops in London.
27 Jun 1944	Cherbourg captured.
9 Jul 1944	Caen captured.
17 Jul 1944	Rommel wounded when his car is bombed.
20 Jul 1944	Assassination attempt on Hitler.
3 Aug 1944	Rennes captured.
13-20 Aug 1944	German Seventh Army defeated in Falaise Gap.
15 Aug 1944	British landings on French Riviera.
17 Aug 1944	Orleans, Chartres and Falaise captured.
25 Aug 1944	Gen. Charles de Gaulle enters Paris.
3 Sep 1944	Germans evacuate Belgium.
4 Sep 1944	Allies capture Antwerp, Brussels, Mons and Abbeville.
8 Sep 1944	First V2 Rocket falls in Britain. Liège captured.
10 Sep 1944	Churchill and Roosevelt in conference in Quebec. US forces enter Luxembourg.
11 Sep 1944	Americans enter Germany near Trier.
12 Sep 1944	Germans in Le Havre surrender.
17 Sep 1944	British airborne forces land at Eindhoven and Arnhem.
28 Sep 1944	Calais captured by Canadians.
3 Oct 1944	Canadians reach River Maas.
14 Oct 1944	Death of Field Marshal Erwin Rommel.
23 Oct 1944	Allies recognise de Gaulle's administration as the provisional government in France.
3 Nov 1944	Flushing captured by Allies. Antwerp re-opened as a port.
24 Nov 1944	Strasbourg captured.
16 Dec 1944	Battle of the Bulge begins and lasts until 5 Jan.
31 Dec 1944	Hitler states Germans will never surrender.
3 Jan 1945	US Army counter-attack on Ardennes Salient.
17 Jan 1945	Russians capture Warsaw.
4-11 Feb 1945	Churchill, Roosevelt and Stalin at Yalta Conference.
8 Feb 1945	Canadian army offensive of Nijmegen, towards the Rhine.
13 Feb 1945	RAF raid on Dresden.
15 Feb 1945	British reach the Rhine.
23 Feb 1945	US forces cross the River Roer.
7 Mar 1945	Cologne captured.
13 March 1945	Allies command West bank of Rhine from Nijmegen to Coblenz.
20 Mar 1945	Mainz, Worms and Kaiserlautern captured.
23 Mar 1945	Rhine crossing.
28 Mar 1945	Last of the 1,050 rockets falls on Britain.
29 Mar 1945	Russians enter Austria. Mannheim captured.
1 Apr 1945	Germans evacuate Holland.
10 Apr 1945	Hanover captured.
11 Apr 1945	Brunswick and Essen captured.
12 Apr 1945	Franklin D. Roosevelt dies.
14 Apr 1945	Arnhem captured.
19 Apr 1945	Leipzig captured.
20 Apr 1945	Russians reach Berlin. Nuremberg captured.
26 Apr 1945	Bremen and Stettin captured. Russians and Americans link up near Torgau on the Elbe.
28 Apr 1945	Allies cross the River Elbe.
29 Apr 1945	Death of Mussolini. Munich captured.
30 Apr 1945	Adolf Hitler dies in Berlin bunker.
1 May 1945	Surrender of German Army in Italy.
2 May 1945	Berlin surrenders to the Russians.
3 May 1945	Allies enter Hamburg.
7 May 1945	German Gen. Jodl capitulates to Eisenhower near Rheims.
8 May 1945	VE – VICTORY IN EUROPE – DAY

Foreword

by Lady Mark Fitzalan Howard

President of the Royal School of Needlework

The Overlord Embroidery commemorates another cross-channel invasion in the opposite direction to that depicted in the Bayeux Tapestry. It is a historical record of the events leading up to and surrounding the second successful armed crossing of the English Channel since the Roman invasion of Britain in 43 A.D. It is 83 metres in length; 12½ metres longer than the Bayeux Tapestry. It consists of 34 panels, each approximately 1 metre high and 2½ metres long.

The Overlord Embroidery was conceived by Lord Dulverton in the 1960's, and the first moves over its execution were started in 1968. It is a tribute to the effort made by the Allies during the 1939-45 War, tracing the planning and historical developments leading up to Operation OVERLORD from 1940 until the invasion of Normandy on 6 June 1944, and the Battle of Normandy in August of that year. Lord Dulverton has said of the Embroidery, which he has given to the nation:

'The sequence of events which the Embroidery portrays was military, and military action of one sort or another is vividly portrayed in practically all of the panels. The armed might of Britain and her allies in this operation does, I think, emerge as forcefully as a limited series of still pictures is likely to be able to convey. The success of the landing and the vast complexity of the preparations, the inter-service and inter-allied co-operation which were a vital and necessary part of the operation can really only be hinted at. We have simply tried to include as many of the salient features as it seemed possible to do. Likewise it has only been possible to hint at the bitterness of the contest and the losses sustained.

We have paid tribute, and rightly, to the leadership and generalship which guided and planned the operation. But the purpose was not to boast of the efficiency of our high command or of the might of our forces in the air and on the sea. The main intention was, and has always been, to pay tribute to the effort and to the sacrifice, of our allies and of our countrymen especially. Everyone was involved to some degree. The fighting services were obviously involved, but the fighting services were made up of "civvies" from all conceivable walks of life, whilst the professionals who taught them what to do and how to do it, were very much in the minority.

*1940 World War 2. Following retreat from Dunkirk, Britain and
Commonwealth stand alone against the threat of Nazi domination of Europe,
and begin, with civilian help, to replenish their industrial and military strength.*

Whatever freedom we now possess to live our lives and shape our destinies and our society, we would not have possessed but for the efforts and the sacrifices which overcame the outrage and the threat of Nazism.

It is to our country and our countrymen, and not to the engines of war which feature in it, that this Embroidery is proudly and humbly dedicated.'

Lord Dulverton commissioned the Embroidery from the Royal School of Needlework in 1968. The designer was Miss Sandra Lawrence, who worked with guidance from an advisory committee comprising the late Air Chief Marshal Sir Donald Evans, Admiral Sir Charles Madden and General Sir Charles Jones. They chose the subject of each panel, with the help of Service Historians from the Ministry of Defence.

Sandra Lawrence prepared small drawings, using war time photographs as reference material to ensure authenticity. She then painted full size cartoons.

The panels were made by stretching strong cotton fabric onto wooden frames, with a durable background linen placed on top. The two layers were then sewn firmly together. Each scene was traced onto the linen by pricking the outlined design and rubbing powder, a mixture of charcoal and cuttlefish, through the perforations. Materials were then cut to the required shapes, placed in position, sewn down and finally edged with cords or cotton couching threads. This method of embroidery is appliqué or applied needlework. Apart from a variety of needles, fine stilettos were the only needlework tools employed, piercing the background fabric, enabling the ends of the cords to be threaded through.

Approximately 50 different materials were used in the Embroidery, including khaki uniform cloth, gold braid, and even a paratrooper's actual beret. Fine or loosely woven fabrics were backed with vilene to give body and to prevent fraying. The silk faces, with features indicated by means of block cast shadows embroidered in long and short stitch, were worked separately in small frames before being applied.

Twenty embroiderers at the Royal School of Needlework were involved in the work. The embroidery was started in the middle of each panel along the entire 2½ metre length, and to facilitate this, the unworked portion at the top and bottom was rolled up. As the needlework progressed, so the background was unwound. Although several embroiderers worked together on each panel, and two or three panels were embroidered simultaneously, it took five years before the task was completed, in 1973.

The result is a work of outstanding merit and historical importance.

I. Prelude

Churchill called it 'Britain's finest hour' but for most of the population, including the troops who had been miraculously saved from the debacle of Dunkirk, 1940 was a year of gloom. Standing alone, bled nearly dry, and daily expecting an invasion across the few brief miles of sea, it seemed inconceivable that one day the tides of war would turn and from this island would be launched the greatest operation in military history. It cannot be too strongly emphasised, there never was nor will be again a campaign involving so many men as OVERLORD. But some four years were to pass before the great reverse could be launched.

The formation of the Commandos, whose first operation was on 22 June 1940 – just two weeks after the British withdrawal from Dunkirk – gave a boost to morale at a time when it was most needed, although the reconnaisance raid they carried out on Boulogne on this date achieved little materially. Otherwise, 1940 was a time for licking wounds, for turning the wheels of industry for the production of vital war materials.

Conscription had been introduced in 1938 and now each month or so brought call-up papers to men in further age groups.

1940 The entire community of Britain bends its will to the war effort. Men, women and children work round the clock. Meanwhile, the Battle of Britain is fought for command of the air over southern England.

At sea, Hitler's U-boats did their best to bring Britain to starvation but still the convoys came through, frequently battered and depleted.

PANEL 2

'As England, in spite of her helpless military position, has shown herself unwilling to come to any compromise I have decided to begin preparations for, and if necessary to carry out, the invasion of England . . . 'The English Air Force must be eliminated to such an extent that it will be incapable of putting up any substantial opposition to the invading troops.'

Thus declared Adolf Hitler in June 1940, words that opened what was to become known as the Battle of Britain. At that time Britain's fate lay in the hands of 1,243 men, the fighter pilots of the RAF.

All through that summer, the skies above South-East England were a battlefield with hundreds of aircraft engaged in dog-fights. On Monday, 16 September, the *Daily Herald* carried as its lead story:

Goering's air force had lost 175 machines up to ten o'clock last night following a day which saw the fiercest air battles of the war. Fighters brought down 171 and AA fire 4.

Thirty British fighters were brought down, but ten of the pilots were safe.

The Battle of Britain had been won by the

Fordson 3-ton winch lorry used for balloon barrage.

Improvised armoured car based on 30-cwt Bedford chassis.

Local Defence Volunteer, (Home Guard) formed 1940.

1940/41 The Blitz. The Luftwaffe concentrates on bombing British cities – killing many thousands of civilians. In London people shelter in tube stations while firemen and air raid wardens fight the 2nd Great Fire.

1941/42 A fierce and remorseless battle is waged in the Atlantic, including a depth charge attack on a U-boat, keeping the convoy routes open, aided by Canadian and Allied navies. From the end of 1941, American troops arrive in Britain and join in the battle which continues into the Spring of 1942. A Home Guard is raised in 1940 as an anti-invasion force.

1941/42 The war is carried into Germany by night with the R.A.F. Lancaster Bombers and by day with unescorted formations of American Fortress Bombers. Fighters return to refuel while Bomber crews are debriefed.

Hurricanes and Spitfires of the Royal Air Force and Hitler was forced to abandon his plans for the invasion of this country – Operation SEA LION, and the air war was about to take a new form.

The air raid on London on the night of 25/26 August 1940, marking the beginning of the Blitz, was carried out by German airmen contrary to the orders of higher command. Harried as they were by Anti-Aircraft guns and by RAF fighters, they abandoned their specified targets and haphazardly dropped their bombs where they could. Supposing that the raid was carried out in accordance with official German policy, RAF Bomber Command retaliated with a raid on Berlin.

On 6 September the Germans decided on a full-scale reprisal raid on London. The following afternoon, Reichmarshal Hermann Goering sent some 300 bombers, escorted by 600 fighters, across the Channel and the Londoner's ordeal by fire began. Before the end of the war eighteen thousand tons of high explosive and incendiary bombs were to fall on the nation's capital leaving an indelible memory on those who lived through it. But out of this suffering came remarkable spirit and courage, and for some, the Blitz brought a heightened sense of community and excitement.

Although raids continued spasmodically, the end of

the Blitz 'proper' came for London on 10 May 1941, the night when the capital burned with over 2,000 fires and 1,436 people died. A quarter of a million books were burnt in the Library of the British Museum. Westminster Abbey, the Tower of London and the

Southern Command truck; Bedford 4x2 GS 3-ton.

Mint were also damaged.

This was the moment when Hitler turned his wrath to the Russians and, just as the Blitz had ended the Battle of Britain, so the German invasion of Russia ended the Blitz.

In retrospect, 1941 can be seen as the year when the Axis powers overstretched and started on the road to decline. On 2 June Germany invaded the USSR in violation of the neutrality pact between them. At first the Red Army were forced back but they eventually sapped the aggressor's strength.

Later that year, on 7 December, the Japanese bombed the US naval base at Pearl Harbour, thus bringing the USA into the war against the Axis.

The resulting alliance of Britain-USSR-USA, to put them in order of involvement, was a strange one, often with seething distrust and even positive dislike below the surface. The summit conferences starting with Washington in December 1941, were very different from the images presented. Firstly, the British Prime Minister, Churchill, had no love for the Russian leader, Josef Stalin, and although there was this immediate need to eradicate the Nazi menace, Churchill made no secret that he felt the further east the Russians were kept the better it would be. To this end, he favoured a drive up through Italy or the Balkans when the time came to invade Europe. There was also a little

1942 Whilst severe fighting ensues in Africa and S.E. Asia, Lord Louis Mountbatten is appointed Chief of Combined Operations. Plans for the invasion of Europe are developed, and full-scale exercises are held.

matter of the non-aggression pact that had existed between Germany and Russia, at the time when Britain stood alone. Roosevelt, the US President, on the other hand, felt in some ways more in harmony with Stalin, having a common dislike of British Imperialism. He also shared the Russian's view that the invasion of Europe should come from the west. Stalin's demands were simple and direct – he wanted a Second Front in the west and wanted it now to relieve the pressure on his own country and, at the same time, screamed out for arms and material supplies which could be ill-afforded by Britain.

In the event, Stalin and Roosevelt had much their own way; but the invasion was not to come as early as they would have liked. Stalin wanted it then, in 1941, and Roosevelt aimed at an invasion of France in the autumn of 1942. Both the dates were quite impracticable. In no way could sufficient build-up of forces and equipment be made in the available time.

War indeed makes for strange bedfellows!

Despite the undeniable courage of the bomber crews, the air war was not a completely glorious record. Too many beautiful cities on both the mainland of Europe and in England were devastated by bombing, often without justifiable cause, and sometimes under the excuse 'baedeker' retaliation.

Such is the organised vandalism of war.

II. Build-up

'We are not allies. We have plenty of allies among the United Nations, but we who are to undertake this great operation are one indivisible force.'
General Eisenhower to his staff, December 1943

PANEL 6
In his book *Normandy to the Baltic*, Field Marshal Montgomery described the object of OVERLORD thus:

To mount and carry out an operation, with forces and equipment established in the United Kingdom and with target date 1 May 1944, to secure a lodgement on the Continent from which further offensive operations could be developed. The lodgement area must contain sufficient port facilities to maintain a force of some twenty-six to thirty divisions and enable that force to be augmented by follow-up shipments from the United States or elsewhere of additional divisions and supporting units at the rate of three to five divisions per month.

This was the essence of the Grand Plan that had been evolved in 1942 by a planning team under the direction of the British Lieutenant-General Sir Frederick Morgan who held the newly created position

of Chief of Staff to the Supreme Allied Commander (COSSAC).

By common consent, the Supreme Commander of OVERLORD would be an American because most of the forces involved would be American. The man selected was General Dwight D. Eisenhower who was US Commander in North Africa: it was there that he met the General who was to be his Commander of Ground Forces, Sir Bernard Law Montgomery. On New Year's Eve 1943, the two men met at Marrakech and first saw the COSSAC plan for OVERLORD.

The choice of the particular Normandy area, between the Contentin peninsular and the Bay of the

British 4x4 staff car; the Humber Heavy Utility.

1943 Meanwhile in France Rommel strengthens the coastal fortifications known as the Atlantic Wall. The local French Resistance sabotage and disrupt German communications, assisted by Allied secret agents.

Seine was influenced by several considerations. Initially the coast around Calais seemed to be a suitable location because of its short distance from England in terms of sea miles and flying time. But the Germans could also see the sense of this choice and had amassed considerable forces in the area.

The alternatives were to look to the north and to the south-west. The north, in Flanders, was dismissed as the ground was too vulnerable to defence flooding. That left the south-west, the area eventually selected.

Volkswagen in military service; the Kfz 1 Kubelwagen.

It had several advantages; it was, in part, sheltered from Atlantic gales by the Contentin peninsula, and there was the nearby port of Cherbourg which would be needed for supplying the forces, and the bonus that the area could be cut off from German reinforcements in the east, simply by bombing the thirty odd bridges over the Seine.

Thus the scene was set, and the build-up for OVERLORD began. Through the Spring of 1944 the Allied forces were training and preparing for D-Day and there was an increasing awareness that the offensive could only be weeks away.

The beaches that had been chosen for the OVERLORD landings are wide and sandy. Behind them are drained salt marshes or sand-dunes. Only between the Vire and the town of Arromanches, a distance of some 20 miles, are there cliffs with 100 feet steep drops into the sea. But these cliffs are broken in two places: by the harbour of Port-en-Bessin and by the beach of Vierville. It was here, code named OMAHA, that the Americans were to make one of their two landings.

Inland there is the *bocage*, a Norman word meaning copse. It is a countryside of hedges on earth banks enclosing irregularly shaped fields. The twenty miles of cliff and the *bocage* formed some natural

French Resistance worker with parachute-dropped sten gun.

*1944 Warships, merchantmen and other vessels assemble in Channel ports.
Paratroops and glider pilots are briefed and trained. Soldiers move into
assembly camps. Tanks are marshalled near the south coast.*

advantages to the defenders, particularly the *bocage* which was to prove an expensive obstacle to the Allies attempting to break out of the bridgehead.

Field Marshal Erwin Rommel returned to Europe from North Africa late in 1943, at first to command an Army Group in Bavaria and Northern Italy but was soon given the task of inspecting the coastal defences of what the Germans called the Atlantic Wall. What he found was alarming; for the most part defences were non-existent. Admittedly around the large ports there were heavy guns and forces of troops for their protection, but elsewhere the Wall comprised a few mines and strands of barbed wire.

In his attempts to improve the position, Rommel applied for and was granted the command of Army Group B – the German Armies stationed between the Netherlands and the Loire, directly subordinate to Field Marshal von Rundstedt commanding Army Group West.

Rommel predicted that the Allied attack, when it came, would be launched against that part of the French coast around the mouth of the Somme. It was in this area, as well as in Normandy, that he decided to concentrate efforts to build up defences.

The 'Wall' that Rommel quickly effected was intended to stop the invaders on the beaches. In the tidal area there were driven huge beams inclined towards the sea, and tipped with steel spikes to hole landing craft or with mines. In the sea itself concrete obstructions were built with naval mines anchored in the shallow water. 'Element C' was a mixed bag of tricks with fences of iron and ferro-concrete erections, all intended to blow up or impede the progress of invading men and vehicles. Of course, there were the conventional minefields and the beach areas covered by a miscellany of armaments encased in concrete bunkers.

In from the shore troops were dug-in in deep entrenchments, and possible landing fields sprouted 'Rommel's asparagus' – heavy posts intended to wreck the Allied gliders, when they landed.

When the invasion came, Rommel's defensive preparations were only about twenty per cent completed.

Certainly, the French Resistance was of considerable help to the Allies at the time of the Normandy landings, but its effectiveness depended on arms, equipment and guidance provided from across the Channel. The British Government had been encouraging and fostering the Resistance since the debacle of 1940. It had to be a softly-softly enterprise as any large-scale organisation would have laid it open to discovery by the Gestapo, with brutal reprisals.

The operation from London consisted of the dropping and landing by Lysander aircraft of specialist agents to contact the Resistance and advise on subversive activities that would have the greatest effect. The agents' brief was a roaming one with no fixed territories and instructions to avoid political affiliations and not to attempt to form chains of command and subordination.

Many agents were French citizens who were brought out of occupied France, trained in Britain, and returned to the continent. On D-Day there were some 300 such agents working with the French Resistance. Their duty had been hazardous during the occupation years; there were 64 known Gestapo victims and no fewer than 297 of their number simply disappeared.

As D-Day approached so Resistance activities were accelerated, with sabotage of railways, telephone services, and ambush of German road transport. Other important Resistance work was the demolition or neutralising of electrical generating plants and factories in production for the Germans.

In the three months before D-Day, 1,500 tons of equipment and arms were air-dropped into France, in addition to about 150 men; from D-Day until the end of August 1944, these numbers were increased to 6,500 and 400 respectively.

1944 The Overlord Commanders meet. Shown, left to right: General Bradley, Admiral Ramsay, Air Chief Marshal Tedder, General Eisenhower, General Montgomery, Air Chief Marshal Leigh-Mallory, General Bedell Smith.

JUNE 1944 Invasion forces sealed in their camps under stringent security procedures make last minute preparation for Operation OVERLORD, while General Montgomery addresses his troops. All the docks are busy; a merchant ship is being loaded. King George VI inspects some of the Naval Ships Company about to embark in readiness for the command to set sail.

Added to this support for the Resistance the Allies, during OVERLORD, introduced other means of assistance. The 'Jedburgh' teams, small groups of French, British and American personnel to guide air drop supplies behind the German lines, where and when needed. The other back-up was the Special Air Service task forces, some 1,900 British and French officers and men who were parachuted in to carry out specific tasks.

Operation NEPTUNE, the Naval part of OVER-LORD comprised two Task Forces: 'West' to land and support the US land forces on OMAHA and UTAH beaches, and 'East' for the British beaches of GOLD, JUNO and SWORD.

Each beach was allocated a Force Headquartership, and each Beach Force was known by an appropriate letter: Force O, Force U, Force G, Force J and Force S.

Apart from these Assault Forces, there was also a Naval Bombarding Force for each sector.

American troops for the D-Day landings were mainly assembled in the West of England, whereas the British and Canadians assembled around Southampton and eastward.

As each of the ships were loaded with heavy stores,

so they moved out to anchor offshore to await the final assembly for the Channel crossing.

The American Ninth Air Force and the British 2nd Tactical Air Force had been formed and equipped for the cover and support of the Naval and ground forces engaged in OVERLORD. But Eisenhower needed something more to attack the communication links between Germany and France. In the Spring of 1944, he succeeded in having the US Eighth Air Force and RAF Bomber Command seconded to his control. Both had been engaged in bombing German industrial targets and now, in their new role, were highly successful in attacking the railways linking France with Germany. During their operations over 1,500 French railway engines were destroyed, a considerable contribution to keeping down the number of German troops in Normandy.

Other targets for Bomber Command and the Eighth were the road bridges over the river Seine. In this they were, to all practical purposes, completely successful.

The bombers also played their part in the deception exercise of Operation FORTITUDE intended to persuade the Germans that the invasion would take place in the Pas de Calais area. Targets there were bombed

Bedford 15-cwt 4x2 GS truck in Royal Navy livery.

and the deception was backed up by dummy landing craft on the Thames and Medway and dummy gliders on Kentish airfields. General Patton's 2nd US Army, which was to be used as a follow-up force, was based in Kent, adding to the general illusion.

As early as February 1944, the British Isles were virtually sealed from the rest of the world, particularly from neutral countries where German Intelligence operators abounded. Then, in April a 10-mile strip of coast all the way round from the Wash to Lands End

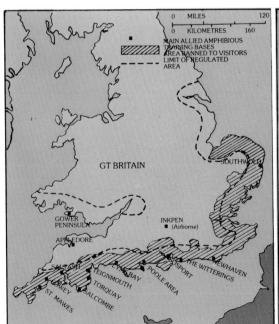

Areas of Britain sealed off prior to D-Day. Certain areas of Scotland were also restricted.

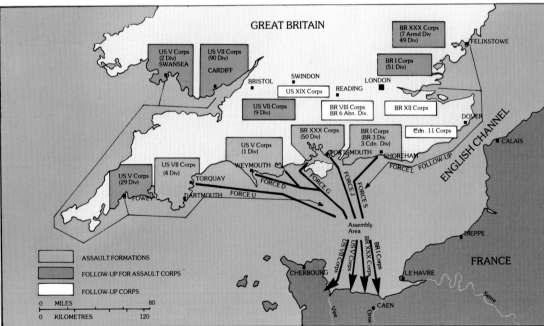

Disposition of forces in Britain and cross-Channel routes.

5th JUNE 1944 This was the original date for D-Day landing, but the bad weather forced a postponement for 24 hours. Here British soldiers of 3rd Division and 27th Armoured Brigade await their sailing order.

Light utility Austin for Lines of Communications units.

Ford 4x2 Heavy Utility 53rd (Welsh) Division.

was closed to visitors. Postal and telephone services were severely cut and any overseas mail censored.

In May at ports all over the country, merchant ships and Naval landing craft were loaded with the hardware needed for this massive amphibious operation.

The troops to take part in the D-Day assault of Operation OVERLORD were 'sealed' in the embarkation camps on 1 June. Tight security meant they had no contact with the outside world and they were not permitted to send letters or make telephone calls.

An advance of £1 or so in French francs was issued as was a gilt coloured tin of emergency food – a chocolate flavoured compound that swelled when eaten, taking away the pangs of hunger. There were instructions on the tin to the effect that it should only be eaten in dire circumstances and then only one square every few hours.

D-Day was to have been Monday 5 June, but on the Saturday before, the weather broke causing another day's wait in the embarkation camps or afloat for those unlucky enough to have been taken aboard.

'On the ground' quote

The evening before we embarked I took a walk through the vehicle lines, devoid of human attendance.

It would have been good to have gone out to a pub

for a final drink before leaving England's shore, but we were not allowed beyond the area.

A barrage balloon flopped around about 100 feet above the ground, and the DD Shermans and a couple of jeeps stood immobile in the fading light, as if they had been there for years instead of a few days.

I climbed on to one of the tanks and wondered what would be its fate. Perhaps it may even survive for a victory parade through some German city.

The territorial position in Europe, 5 June 1944.

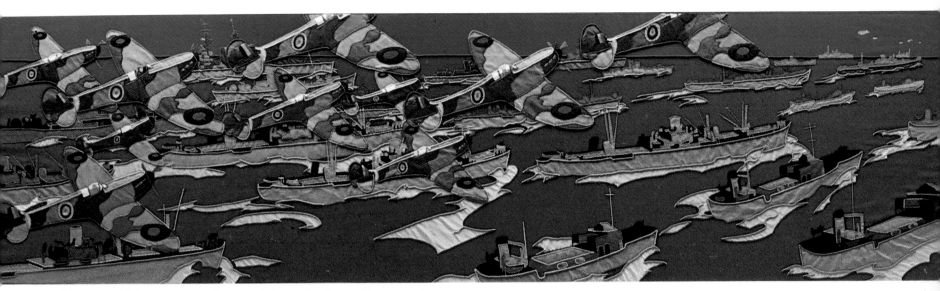

5th JUNE 1944 At dawn on 5th June 1944 the weather forecast improves. The great invasion convoy sets sail, protected by 15 squadrons of fighters. Destroyers and aircraft search for enemy submarines and warships.

III. 'We'll Go'

The fighting ships had begun to move south from their northern bases on 2 June. The following day the convoy which had been assembling off Falmouth sailed for the east.

All was prepared for D-Day on the 5th. However, in the small hours of the 4th Eisenhower had been given a meteorological report forecasting very bad weather, probably lasting for the next three days. At dawn he decided to postpone the venture for 24 hours and ordered the vessels already at sea to return. In fact, the ships of Force U2 could not be contacted by wireless signal and destroyers had to be sent to bring them back.

Sunday, 4 June, was a stormy day and fears grew that it might not be possible to carry out the invasion in the few days when the tides would be right. In the evening, the Supreme Commander learned from his Met. Officer that there was a slim chance of better weather lasting until the evening of the 6th.

The fate of the entire operation was in the balance and Eisenhower had to make one of the most dangerous decisions in military history. By dawn on the 5th he had made up his mind. It was 'We'll go' and the ships were again on the move.

OVERLORD had begun in earnest.

The sheer size of the Operation NEPTUNE part of OVERLORD defies the imagination. A total of 6,939 ships were engaged in the crossing, the number made up by 1,213 Naval Fighting Ships, 4,126 Landing Ships and Craft, 736 Ancillary Ships and Craft, 864 Merchant Ships. 54 small craft, including 20 Rhino ferries or towing craft were lost in the crossing.

It was a near miracle that out of all these vessels the great majority reached the French coast at all, let alone the achievement of arriving at their allotted time, almost to the minute.

'On the ground' quote

I admit I was scared and seasick on the way over. What the hell would be waiting for us? I kept thinking – 'Well, the Army feeds us at regular intervals, and the way to face this is to take the intervals between meals as those of danger'... Get through the time between breakfast and lunch and between lunch and the evening meal, and I'll be alright.

In the event, of course, meals did not come at regular intervals and there was that terrible moment on the third day when almost all the platoon were wiped out by mortar shell while scoffing Maconochies, before starting on the treacle pudding.

The minesweepers were in sight of the French coast early in the evening of the 5th, their sweeping duty taking them sufficiently close to shore to be able to recognise houses, but the Germans ignored them.

German Naval E Boats – fast torpedo vessels – did not appear at this time and were presumably tied up in the harbours of Cherbourg and Le Havre.

The 82nd and 101st US Airborne Divisions, commanded by Major General Matthew B. Ridgeway and Major General Maxwell Taylor respectively, had been ordered to drop on the Contentin peninsular to support the landings on UTAH beach.

The Jeep, 4x4 Command Reconnaissance Truck.

5th JUNE 1944 1,200 warships escort the invasion fleet of 4,200 landing ships and craft, including blockships which will be sunk to form sheltered anchorages. R.A.F. Lancasters fly over to bomb coastal batteries.

5th JUNE 1944 Ahead of the convoys, 12 flotillas of R.N. Minesweepers clear ten channels for the Task Force fleets; two paths for each of the five assault forces heading for the beaches of Normandy. The Germans, not anticipating a landing attempt, do not detect the minesweepers and an early and vital mission of the Operation is successfully accomplished.

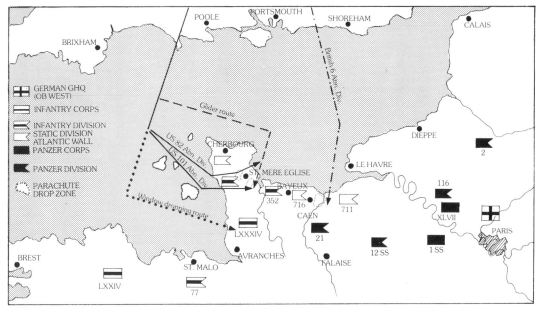

The Fly-in routes and Dropping Zones in Normandy of both British and American Airborne forces.

SS General Dietrich, Commander of 1SS Panzer Corps with one of tank officers.

It was by no means a universally approved plan and some officers on the SHAEF staff had misgivings. The ground for the proposed drop had been flooded as part of Rommel's Atlantic Wall defences, fields which were still dry were mined and, equally bad, the Anti-Aircraft defences were strong in the area.

Of the two divisions, the 82nd was the only one to have been in previous action and had had a parti-cularly rough time supporting the Sicilian landings at Salerno, whereas the 101st had been raised for D-Day and would be going into action for the first time.

About midnight on 2 June, two Royal Navy midget submarines, X20 and X23, left Portsmouth for the French coast, their mission to act as markers showing flashing green beacons seaward off JUNO and SWORD beaches respectively. These submarine craft each carried a crew of two Lieutenants and an engine room artificer, augmented by a Combined Operations pilotage-party of two naval officers.

For the first part of their voyage they were towed by trawlers but for most of the passage they were un-escorted. After identifying the two beaches, they were to submerge and remain hidden. On the morning of D-Day, in darkness, they were to surface and show their beacons as guides for the assault landing craft. The darkness meant any distinguishing features on the

shore were hard to identify, but the task was vital because of the dangerous outcrop of rock in a number of places, and the mud flats where the Orne flows into the sea.

The midget submarines reached the French coast shortly before dawn on Sunday, 4 June, and lay on the bottom until light, when they surfaced to periscope depth in order to take bearings on the shore. Having done so and noting no signs of movement, they anchored and submerged again where they remained for the rest of the day and through the daylight hours of the 5th.

It was at 0508 hours on the 6th that X23 lit her beacon off SWORD beach, closely followed by X20 at JUNO. X23's log read:

'0500. Surfaced and checked position by shore fix in dawn light. Rigged mast with lamp and radar beacon'.

This was 76 hours after leaving Portsmouth, 64 of which had been spent under water, a remarkable test of endurance for the five men in each craft in their extremely cramped conditions.

The Germans undoubtedly felt safe that night, convinced that no invasion force would be capable or mad enough to go to sea in such heavy weather. Field Marshal Rommel had even decided to make a quick visit to Germany to celebrate his wife's birthday.

There was, of course, the drone from the engines of the bombers of the RAF and the USAF, but there was nothing unusual in that – they had been attacking coastal targets for months.

The brief of the 82nd US Airborne Division was to isolate the western flank of the invasion by taking the crossroads at Ste-Mere-Eglise and by capturing or destroying bridges over the rivers Merderet and Douve. The task of their compatriots in the 101st was to take the town of Carentan and keep open the landward roads for the seaborne forces.

Pathfinders of the American Airborne Divisions took off two hours before midnight on the 5th. Because of low cloud over Normandy the aircraft navigators were unable to visually check their positions and, in consequence, the Pathfinders parachuted some way off their planned Dropping Zones, and had to set up their Eureka radios and lights where they landed. Unfortunately, the same navigational problem beset the main airborne force resulting in confusion of regiments landing in the wrong DZs. Other parachutists were scattered over an area of several hundred square miles.

However, all was not lost and everywhere the airborne men were fighting battles as individuals or in small groups, eventually linking up into larger groups

5th JUNE 1944 Airborne forces depart to capture vital bridges and gun
batteries. General Eisenhower briefs 82nd and 101st U.S. Airborne Divisions.
Paratroops of the British 6th Airborne Division synchronise watches.

5th/6th JUNE 1944 An elaborate deception plan persuades the Germans of an
invasion in the area around the Pas de Calais. Thus the German troops are
unaware of imminent invasion and certainly do not expect any such attempt in
the prevailing weather conditions. Despite all hazards a British midget submarine
surfaces off the coast to identify the invasion beaches by showing a green light.

5th/6th JUNE 1944 Just after midnight of 5th June, the first paratroopers and gliders land. Seaborne commandos led by the piper of their Brigadier Lord Lovat link up with the paratroopers on the afternoon of 6th June.

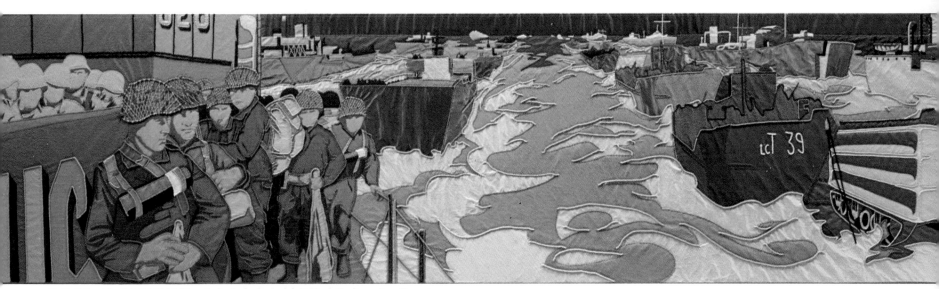

D-DAY – 6th JUNE 1944 Shortly before dawn on D-Day the invasion fleet assembles off the Normandy coast. Despite rough weather there has been remarkably little loss and the estimated time for the arrival and initial assault has proved extremely accurate. Assault landing craft are lowered and head for the beaches.

Commando in webbing kit with canvas ammunition carrier.

and achieving most of their original objectives, one of which was the town of Ste-Mere-Eglise, which was taken at approximately 0400 hours, on the 6th. The cost was high: something like 20 per cent casualties.

The British 6th Airborne Division, commanded by Major General Sir Richard Gale, was given the task of taking or destroying the bridges on the eastern flank of the beaches, on the high ground between the rivers Orne and Dives. In particular the bridges over the Orne and the Caen Canal had to be captured before the Germans could destroy them.

In the first few minutes of D-Day, gliders carrying men of the 2nd Battalion Oxfordshire and Buckinghamshire Light Infantry and sappers, under the command of Major John Howard, crash-landed in a field close to the bridge, breaking the wings off the gliders on Rommel's 'asparagus' posts as they did so. The Major's glider came to rest a bare fifty yards from the Canal Bridge closely followed by two other gliders of his force. Completely surprised, the German defenders of the bridge were overwhelmed and the bridge taken and held despite German counter-attacks. This was to become known as Pegasus Bridge, after the Airborne forces' insignia emblem, and it was here, in the afternoon of D-Day that men of the 1st SS (Commando) Brigade, led by Bill Millin, the personal piper of the commander, Lord Lovat, joined up with Major Howard's tired but successful force.

Like the situation in the American Zones, things went wrong for the British paratroops; bad drops resulting in men being scattered over wide areas. However, most objectives were achieved, albeit with substantial cost.

IV. The Beaches

'Believe me, Lang, the first 24 hours of the invasion will be decisive . . . for the Allies, as well as for Germany, it will be the longest day!'
Field-Marshal Rommel to his aide-de-camp, April 1944

The troopships had been arriving at their assembly points since midnight, and everything was going according to plan despite the heavy seas.

The landing craft left the main fleet to head for the beaches. From the craft, amphibious tanks were launched, but some of them were swamped before reaching the shore.

The Bombarding Forces of Operation NEPTUNE were, with the bombing by the combined Allied Air Forces, intended to soften up the German defences prior to the landings of assault troops. The western

L.V.T. Mk 4; Alligator or Water Buffalo.

Horsa troop carrying glider; used in OVERLORD.

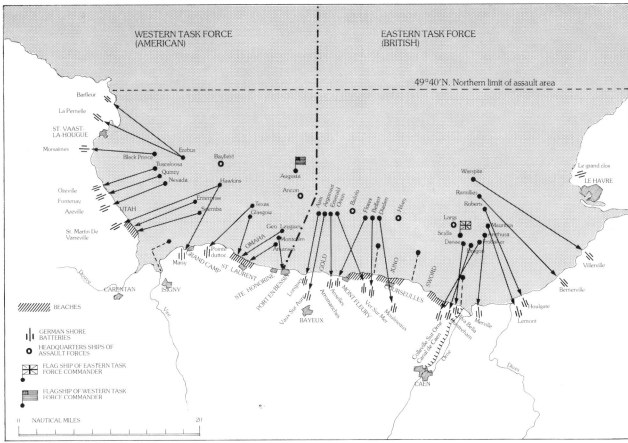

WESTERN TASK FORCE
(AMERICAN)

EASTERN TASK FORCE
(BRITISH)

49°40'N. Northern limit of assault area

Barfleur

La Pernelle

ST. VAAST-
LA-HOUGUE

Morsalines

Black Prince   Erebus   Bayfield

Tuscaloosa
Quincy
Nevada   Hawkins   Augusta

Ozeville   Ancon

Fontenay   Texas   Ajax
Azeville   Enterprise   Glasgow   Argonaut   Baldio
        Somba   Emerald   Flores
UTAH   Orion   Ballast
                        Geo. Leygue   Dakdon   Hilay
St. Martin De
Varreville   Montcalm

                Pointe   Arkansas
        Maisy   duttoc.
              GRAND CAMP   ST. LAURENT   OMAHA

        CARENTAN   ISIGNY   STE. HONORINE

Warspite

Ramillies
Roberts   Le grand clos
                              LE HAVRE

Largs
Scylla   Mauritius
Danae   Arethusa
      Frobisher
        Argonaut   Villerville

Bernerville

Houlgate
                Lemont

BEACHES

GERMAN SHORE
BATTERIES

HEADQUARTERS SHIPS OF
ASSAULT FORCES

FLAG SHIP OF EASTERN TASK
FORCE COMMANDER

FLAGSHIP OF WESTERN TASK
FORCE COMMANDER

0   NAUTICAL MILES   20

Bayeux   Vaux Sur Aure   Amelies   Arromanches   MONT FLEURY   Ver Sur Mer   Moulineaux   COURSEULLES   JUNO   SWORD   Luc   La Bella   Ouistreham   Merville

Colleville Sur Orne   Canal de Caen   Orne   Dives

CAEN

Targets of the Naval Bombardment Forces at 05.30 – 08.00 hours on D-Day, showing the position of forces and naval vessels.

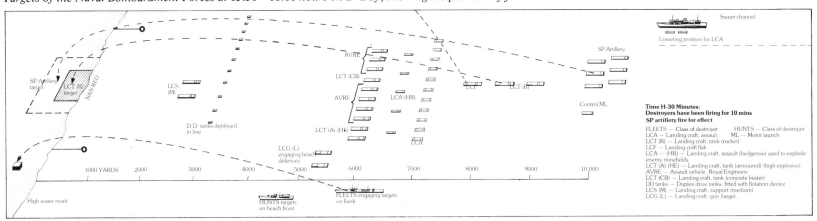

Swept channel

Lowering position for LCA

SP Artillery

AVRE

LCT (CB)

SP Artillery
target   LCT (R)
              target   LCS
                            (M)   AVRE   LCA (HR)   LCF   LCT (R)

                        D.D. tanks deployed
                        in line   Control ML

                                LCT (A) (HE)

                                        LCA

                        LCG (L)
                        engaging beach
                        defences

High water mark

1000 YARDS   2000   3000   4000   5000   6000   7000   8000   9000   10,000

        HUNTS targets
        on beach front   FLEETS engaging targets
                              on flank

Time H-30 Minutes:
Destroyers have been firing for 10 mins
SP artillery fire for effect

FLEETS — Class of destroyer   HUNTS — Class of destroyer
LCA — Landing craft, assault.   ML — Motor launch
LCT (R) — Landing craft, tank (rocket)
LCF — Landing craft flak
LCA — (HR) — Landing craft, assault (hedgerow) used to explode
enemy minefields.
LCT (A) (HE) — Landing craft, tank (armoured) (high explosive)
AVRE — Assault vehicle, Royal Engineers
LCT (CB) — Landing craft, tank (concrete buster)
DD tanks — Duplex drive tanks, fitted with flotation device
LCS (M) — Landing craft, support (medium)
LCG (L) — Landing craft, gun (large)

Aerial view of the sea to land fire plan for battleships and the arrangement of all task forces prior to beach landings.

D-DAY – 6th JUNE 1944 Assault craft and amphibious tanks proceed towards the shore in the heavy seas. Many of these tanks founder in the rough sea, and thus it is decided to land most of the others directly onto the beaches.

beaches, UTAH and OMAHA were assigned to Western Task Force, commanded by Rear-Admiral A. G. Kirk aboard the Task flagship USS *Augusta*.

Bombardment Force A had responsibility for UTAH beach, with a complement of 16 ships, including the USS *Nevada*, and USS *Tuscaloosa*, flagship of Force A.

On the left, Bombardment Force C, with sights set on OMAHA beach, was headed by the battleships USS *Texas* (flagship) and USS *Arkansas*. Their strength was made up by 3 cruisers and 11 destroyers.

GOLD, JUNO and SWORD beaches were the responsibility of Eastern Task Force, under the command of Rear-Admiral Sir Philip Vian, in the cruiser HMS *Scylla*. GOLD and JUNO beaches came under the guns of Bombarding Forces K and E respectively. The 18 ships that were assigned to GOLD and 13 to JUNO were mainly destroyers. SWORD beach, however, had the larger Bombardment Force D allocated to it. The destroyer section alone was 13 in number, and their part in the bombardment took place with the ships only a few hundred yards off the shore. Flagships for the Eastern Bombarding Task Force were HMS *Belfast* (Force E), HMS *Mauritius* (Force D), and HMS *Argonaut* (Force K).

In addition to all these regular warships, both task forces had their own reserves, mainly destroyers drawn from escort duty, and as a General Reserve there was the battleship HMS *Nelson*.

Besides these Bombarding Forces, each Naval Assault Force had further backing from an assortment of landing craft specially equipped with various close support weapons.

Before the landings the Bombarding Forces had to rely on direct and aircraft observation for reporting the accuracy of the attack. This was provided by four squadrons of Fleet Air Arm Seafires, five RAF squadrons of Spitfires and Mustangs and US Navy pilots flying 15 Spitfires. Seven aircraft were lost in this

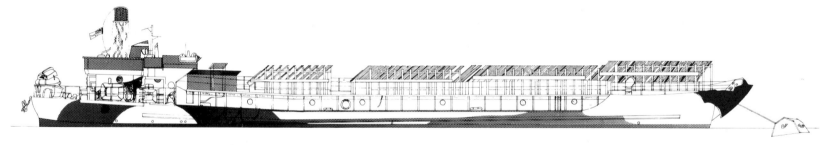

Rocket Landing Craft, which could carry 800 to 1000 5-inch HE rockets.

D-DAY – 6th JUNE 1944 German defences are heavily bombarded by forces firing along a fifty mile front directed by airborne spotters in Mustangs and Spitfires. Coastal command flying boats protect the fleet from German U-Boats.

part of the operation. When the troops were ashore, the air observation was supplemented by F.O.B. (Forward Observation Bombardment) units, made up of specialist Army observers and Naval signallers with radio sets.

The heavy air attack that complemented the bombardment from the sea involved the night raiding of the planes from RAF Bomber Command and some sixteen hundred bombing aircraft of the US 8th and 9th Air Forces. On UTAH beach, the final bombing by 269 low flying Marauders took place only ten minutes before the landing of the troops and was generally successful.

On OMAHA and on the British front the situation was complicated by poor visibility and the bombers had to use the alternative plan of flying in line abreast formation and bombing under the orders of path-finders. OMAHA was attacked by 329 high flying Liberators, which, because of low cloud, had the complication of risking the hitting of incoming landing craft. In consequence, bombs were dropped well off target and were scattered up to three miles inland.

The coastal air bombardment overall was perhaps only partially successful but it had the effect of keeping the defending German troops under cover

until 10 minutes before H-Hour.

The assault on UTAH beach in the American sector was the responsibility of the 4th Infantry Division of VII Corps, commanded by Major-General J. L. Collins, carried in 865 ships and craft provided and commanded by Rear Admiral Don P. Moon, United States Navy.

The Task Force arrived at the assembly area off UTAH beach at 0200 hours on the 6th after a stormy crossing with plenty of seasickness among the troops. First ashore was a contingent of 124 men of the 4th US Cavalry, landing on the small-offshore Iles de Marcouf which were void of the enemy. As the troops moved into the assault landing craft, the beach was being bombarded by Marauders of the Ninth US Air Force and from the sea by the Naval Task Force. Along with the troops went the close-support landing craft equipped with guns and 32 DD tanks provided by the British 79th Armoured Division – 28 of which managed to make the landing.

However, it was by no means a smooth and uneventful operation; the 8th Infantry 2nd Battalion found themselves ashore alright, but something like a mile off their target. The situation was righted by some remarkable leadership on the part of Brig-General Theodore Roosevelt, the Assistant Divisional

Commander who marshalled his forces from the beach. Regrettably, a few days later the General was to die from a heart attack.

UTAH was not an easy landing but by the afternoon and early evening the 4th Division was pushing inland and joining up with the US paratroops who had landed on the previous night.

One of the most adventurous landing actions, and one, unfortunately, omitted from the Overlord Embroidery was that of the Provisional Ranger Force (The US equivalent to British Commandos) commanded by Lt Col James E. Rudder, whose task was to neutralise the heavy artillery battery at Pointe du Hoc jutting out into the Bay of the Seine on the Calvados coast.

The Rangers' attack had to be made up the sheer 100 foot cliff which had been given a liberal dressing of barbed wire and trip flares. Back in Britain, Lt Col Rudder had decided on a frontal storm up the cliff with mortar-fired grappling lines and scaling ladders, and had been exercising the Rangers on the cliffs of the Isle of Wight.

On the day, the assault landing craft carrying the Rangers were spotted by the Germans and shelled by the guns on the shore. But with supporting fire from their escorting destroyer, a landing was made and lines

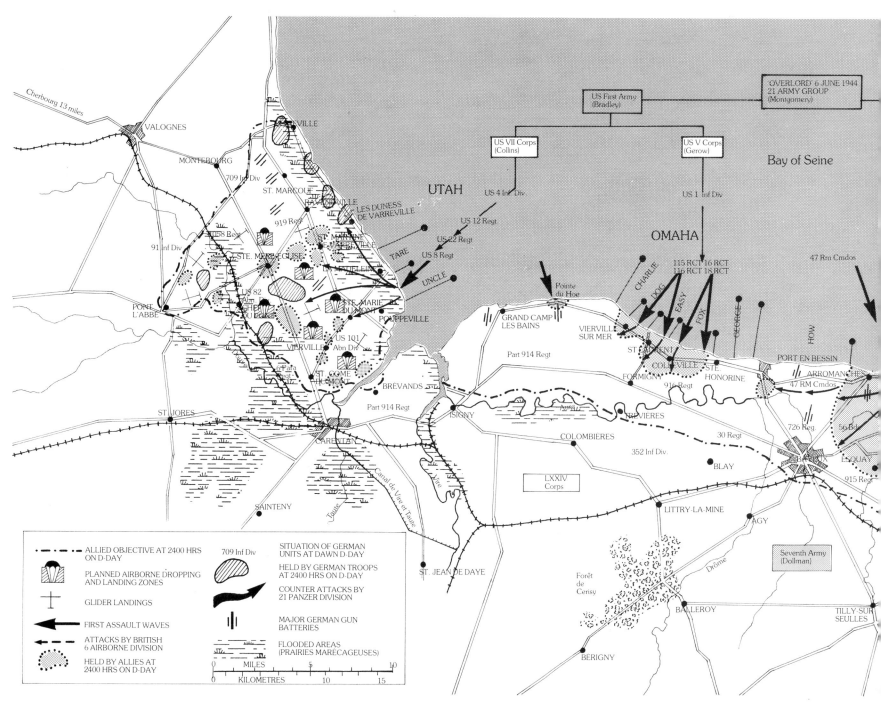

OVERLORD 6 JUNE 1944
21 ARMY GROUP
(Montgomery)

US First Army
(Bradley)

US VII Corps
(Collins)

US V Corps
(Gerow)

Bay of Seine

Cherbourg 13 miles

VALOGNES

MONTEBOURG

709 Inf Div

ST. MARCOUF

RAVENVILLE

LES DUNESS
DE VARREVILLE

919 Regt

ST. MARTIN
DE VARREVILLE

91 Inf Div

1058 Regt

STE. MÈRE-ÉGLISE

TARE

US 12 Regt

US 22 Regt

US 8 Regt

UTAH

US 4 Inf Div

US 1 Inf Div

OMAHA

47 Rm Cmdos

LA HENDELIER

115 RCT   16 RCT
116 RCT   18 RCT

CHARLIE

DOG

EASY

FOX

UNCLE

Pointe
du Hoe

US 82
Abn Div

PONT
L'ABBE

CHEF
DU PONT

STE. MARIE
DU MONT

GRAND CAMP
LES BAINS

VIERVILLE
SUR MER

GEORGE

HOW

PORT EN BESSIN

POUPPEVILLE

ST. LAURENT

COLLEVILLE

STE.
HONORINE

ARROMANCHES

US 101
Abn Div

VIERVILLE

Part 914 Regt

FORMIGNY

916 Regt

47 RM Cmdos

6 Para
Regt

ST. COME
DU MONT

BREVANDS

Part 914 Regt

ISIGNY

TREVIERES

726 Regt

ESQUAY

56 Bd

ST. JORES

CARENTAN

Aure

COLOMBIERES

30 Regt

BAYEUX

915 Regt

352 Inf Div.

BLAY

SAINTENY

Taute

Canal de Vire et Taute

Vire

LXXIV
Corps

LITTRY-LA-MINE

AGY

ST. JEAN DE DAYE

Forêt
de
Cerisy

Drôme

Seventh Army
(Dollman)

BERIGNY

BALLEROY

TILLY-SUR-
SEULLES

Legend:
- - - · - - - ALLIED OBJECTIVE AT 2400 HRS ON D-DAY

709 Inf Div   SITUATION OF GERMAN UNITS AT DAWN D-DAY

PLANNED AIRBORNE DROPPING AND LANDING ZONES

HELD BY GERMAN TROOPS AT 2400 HRS ON D-DAY

GLIDER LANDINGS

COUNTER ATTACKS BY 21 PANZER DIVISION

FIRST ASSAULT WAVES

MAJOR GERMAN GUN BATTERIES

ATTACKS BY BRITISH 6 AIRBORNE DIVISION

FLOODED AREAS (PRAIRIES MARECAGEUSES)

HELD BY ALLIES AT 2400 HRS ON D-DAY

MILES   5   10

KILOMETRES   10   15

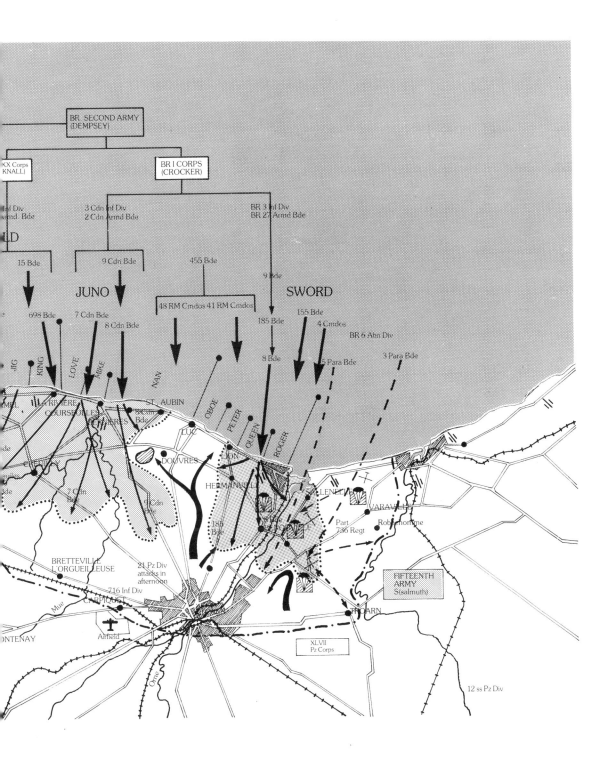

Operation Overlord Code Names

ANVIL Initial name for Allied landings in the South of France in August 1944. Renamed DRAGOON.

BODYGUARD Deceptive plan covering Allied strategy in Europe.

BOLERO United States build-up of forces and supplies for Overlord.

BOMBARDON Floating steel breakwaters of Mulberry harbours.

CORNCOB Blockships forming part of Gooseberry breakwaters.

CROSSBOW Preventive Allied measures against V1 and V2 weapons.

FORTITUDE Cover plan for Overlord, directing attention to the Pas de Calais area.

GOOSEBERRY Artificial breakwaters for Mulberry harbours and offshore anchorages.

MAPLE Mine laying part of Neptune.

MULBERRY Artificial harbours.

NEPTUNE The naval part of Overlord.

PHOENIX Concrete caisson used as breakwaters for Mulberry harbours.

PLUTO Pipe Line Under the Ocean for supplying petrol from England to the continent.

POINTBLANK Offensive by Allied bombers.

RANKIN Contingency plan in the event of German surrender prior to Overlord.

TOMBOLA Pipeline supply of petrol from tankers for storage in Normandy.

WHALE Floating steel pierheads for Mulberry and roadways to shore.

Area and Beach Code Names

GOLD – From eastern extremity of OMAHA beach to the river Provence. The area was divided into three parts: ITEM, JIG and KING beaches.

JUNO – From the eastern extremity of GOLD beach to St Aubin-sur-Mer. The area was divided into three parts. LOVE, MIKE and NAN beaches.

SWORD – From the eastern extremity of JUNO to the river Orne. Parts of the area were code named OBOE, PETER, QUEEN and ROGER. An area to the east of SWORD was code name BAND.

OMAHA – From Carentan estuary to western extremity of GOLD beach.

UTAH – The Cherbourg Peninsular, northwards from the mouth of the river Vire. Parts of the area were named TARE and UNCLE.

D-DAY – 6th JUNE 1944 As the assault troops head for shore, German coastal defences are attacked by bombers. By night there are 1056 Lancasters, Halifaxes and Mosquitoes. By day, 1600 Fortresses, Liberators and Marauders.

shot up the cliffs by the mortars. The ascent was made but by this time the Germans had withdrawn the guns to positions some half a mile inland. Eventually, the guns were destroyed but the Germans counter-attacked. The Rangers were under siege for two days and were relieved by some of the second wave troops from OMAHA beach.

PANEL 23 OMAHA

Aboard the USS *Augusta* at 1000 hours of the 6th, D-Day there was concern. General Omar Bradley, in charge of the American land forces had good news from the UTAH beach; from the Airborne troops, although there had been considerable resistance the objectives must have been gained as the UTAH forces were finding their way through the beach exits; and as the guns on the Pointe du Hoc were now silent, it was reasonable to suppose that the Rangers had done their job. But from OMAHA beach there was nothing but bad news. Reports from General Gerow, the Corps Commander, spoke of heavy casualties and heavy losses of DD Tanks, intensive artillery and machine-gun fire.

OMAHA was probably better protected by the Germans than any other invasion beach. To them it had seemed an obvious place for a landing. The initial occupation of this beach had been entrusted to the 1st Infantry Division commanded by Major-General

A US private wearing camouflage combat dress.

Clarence R. Huebner. In the following wave came the 29th Infantry Division.

The causes behind the trouble were complex; firstly, the invading force was not strong enough to defeat the defenders. Secondly, the assembly area where the troops were to tranship into their assault craft, and where the DD Tanks were to take to the water was all of 12 miles from the landing; the sea was rough and many of the craft and tanks were swamped – 27 of the DDs being lost with most of their crews, and the majority of the troops were suffering from sea-sickness. Most of the beach obstacles were under water and these took heavy toll of the craft and troops.

By noon the position was such that Bradley was considering the evacuation of OMAHA and ordering his follow up forces to land at either UTAH or the British beaches, when came the message 'advancing up heights'.

The men of the 1st were tired of being pinned down and slowly, with losses at every step, they were getting off the beach. To the right, the 29th Division was now ashore and taking heavy punishment, but like the 1st they were also making slow progress inland.

PANELS 24, 25

Because of differences in times of tide the British and Canadian Armies landed on their respective beaches half an hour after the American assault. The

6th JUNE 1944 – UTAH BEACH H-Hour, the landing time, varies from 6.30 to 7.45 a.m. according to tide. Five assault divisions land. The 4th U.S. Division, supported by 28 amphibious tanks, heads inland and joins the airborne forces.

6th JUNE 1944 – OMAHA BEACH The 1st U.S. Division meet determined opposition. Landing craft are swamped and 27 amphibious tanks sink. Heavy enemy fire pins the troops to the beach, where Rommel's mined obstacles are the only available cover. Only after several hours and at a cost of 3,000 casualties, a beachhead of 6 miles wide is secured.

The Atlantic Wall

Although Field Marshal Rommel found, on inspections in early 1944, the Atlantic Wall (coastal defences that extended from the Skagerrak to the Spanish frontier) was inadequate and in some areas simply non-existent, by the end of May it was indeed a formidable obstacle.

The erections on the beaches intended to thwart the assualt craft are described elsewhere but the defences did not stop at the beaches. In Normandy the Wall was, in effect, a strong crust of concrete affording protection for the defenders against bombardment and allowing maximum fire power to be brought to bear on the beaches. Every seaside town was a fortress; villages were booby-trapped and encircled by mines; roads to the seaward were bricked up and guns were mounted in seafront cellars. Sand dunes were tunnelled and concrete bunkers housed the heavy artillery.

Manning the seafront were the German secondary divisions whose task was to hold the invading force and await the arrival of the SS and Panzer troops who were grouped inland in order to move quickly to whichever beaches were under attack.

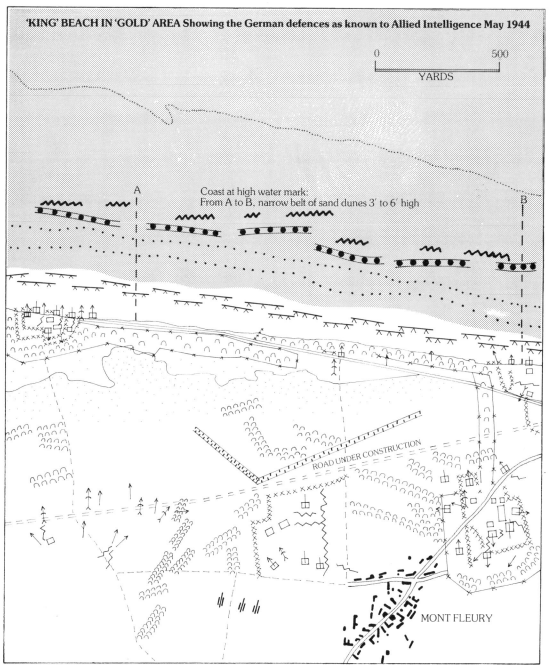

'KING' BEACH IN 'GOLD' AREA Showing the German defences as known to Allied Intelligence May 1944

Coast at high water mark: From A to B, narrow belt of sand dunes 3' to 6' high

ROAD UNDER CONSTRUCTION

MONT FLEURY

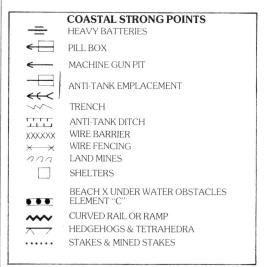

COASTAL STRONG POINTS

≡	HEAVY BATTERIES
⟵▭	PILL BOX
⟵	MACHINE GUN PIT
▭	ANTI-TANK EMPLACEMENT
⟪⟵	TRENCH
⊥⊥⊥⊥	ANTI-TANK DITCH
XXXXXX	WIRE BARRIER
×—×	WIRE FENCING
∩∩∩	LAND MINES
▯	SHELTERS
●●●	BEACH X UNDER WATER OBSTACLES ELEMENT "C"
∿∿	CURVED RAIL OR RAMP
⟋⟍	HEDGEHOGS & TETRAHEDRA
······	STAKES & MINED STAKES

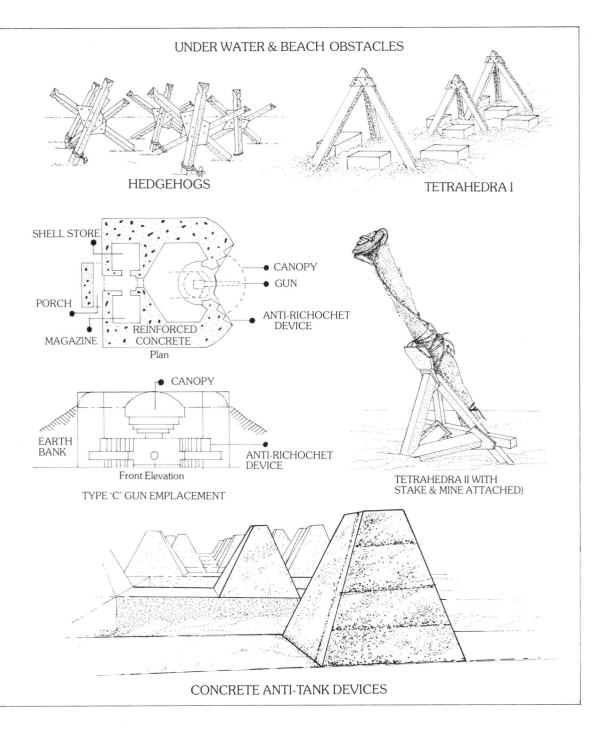

UNDER WATER & BEACH OBSTACLES

HEDGEHOGS

TETRAHEDRA I

SHELL STORE

PORCH

MAGAZINE

CANOPY

GUN

ANTI-RICHOCHET DEVICE

REINFORCED CONCRETE

Plan

CANOPY

EARTH BANK

Front Elevation

ANTI-RICHOCHET DEVICE

TYPE 'C' GUN EMPLACEMENT

TETRAHEDRA II WITH STAKE & MINE ATTACHED)

CONCRETE ANTI-TANK DEVICES

Naval Bombardment had done a good job and the troops were able to gain a sure foothold. However, the German resistance was fierce and as the area was comparatively built up, street-fighting, that slow, slogging style of warfare, was inevitable.

On GOLD beach the 50th (Northumbrian) Division had the task of pushing inland between La Rivière and Le Hamel and to take Arromanches and Bayeux. The Division's 69th and 231st Brigades landed at La Rivière and Le Hamel respectively and found themselves heavily engaged by troops of the German 352nd Division, the same force that was giving so much trouble to the Americans on OMAHA. It was the specialised armour, the 'funnies' of the 79th Armoured Division 'zoo' that greatly helped the British troops to get off the beach but not without heavy casualties. In addition, the use of 'Bangalore Torpedoes' was helping clear the beach of obstructions.

The No. 47 (Royal Marine) Commando had a particularly arduous task although they came ashore two hours after the first landing. Their target was Port en Bessin, a small port on the right extremity of GOLD beach. The idea was to attack the port from the land side and, in order to do this, the Commando would

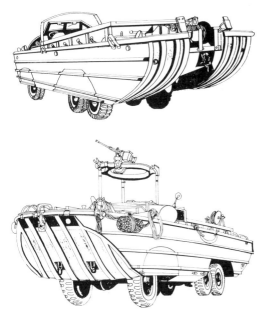

Amphibious truck, 2¼-ton, 6x6, DUKW.

6th JUNE 1944 – GOLD, JUNO, SWORD BEACHES Three assault divisions of British and Canadians progress, although none can gain its final objectives, mainly due to beach obstacles hidden by the high tide. Much equipment and several tanks are lost.

6th JUNE 1944 – GOLD, JUNO, SWORD BEACHES Specialised engineer tanks, which clear minefields, pillboxes, bridge anti-tank ditches and help eliminate enemy strongpoints, are sent in to support the troops; infantry of the 50th British Division on GOLD beach, 3rd Canadian Division on JUNO and 3rd British Division on SWORD. Allied aircraft patrol over the beaches.

have a ten mile march. Unfortunately, when the Commando came ashore they found that the assault troops, in this case the 1st Hampshires were having a bad time, losing the commanding officer and many others of their strength in the engagement. The 47 Commando did not reach Port en Bessin before dark on the 6th and it took another day to capture the town.

To return to the fortunes of the 50th Division. At La Rivière the 69th Brigade landed and advanced inland. One company of the East Yorkshire Regiment was, however, pinned down on the beach and again the assault troops had reason to thank the specialised armour of the 79th for relieving their plight. Similar incidents, great and small, were happening on GOLD throughout the 6th, but by the end of the day the beach was firmly held and the 50th Division, by now well inland, had linked with the Canadians who had landed at JUNO. These were the 3rd Canadian Division and the 2nd Canadian Armoured Brigade. Their aim was to advance inland from the beach and take Carpiquet airfield near Caen. Of course, this was vital if General Montgomery's intention to capture Caen by the evening of the first day was to be realised. In the event, it was not to be until 10 July that Caen would be 'neutralised', and the 18th before all the suburbs were eventually cleared of the enemy.

The Canadians did not have a good start to their day; many of their landing craft were wrecked or blown up on the obstructions and, as they had been delayed by bad weather, the beach at high tide was too narrow for the adequate marshalling of their equipment.

On this beach, like on GOLD, the specialised armour of the 79th gave valuable help to the troops in getting off the beach.

Canadian tanks had, by the afternoon, cut the Caen-Bayeux Road seven miles inland and it seemed that Caen itself by nightfall might yet be possible. But the Germans counter-attacked, thus delaying the impetus and allowing further German reinforcements in the area, and Caen did not fall.

Between the Canadians on JUNO and the British 3rd Division eastward on SWORD was an area allotted to two Royal Marine Commandos: the 41st and the 48th. The brief of the latter was to land at the small village of St. Aubin two hours after the Canadians had made their assault on JUNO, and at the same time 41 (Royal Marine) Commando was to land five miles eastward at Lion-sur-Mer. The two were then to turn to each other and meet, mopping-up the enemy positions as they went. However, events were not to turn out that way; the 49th not only came under

The Specialised Tracked Vehicles, Hobart's 'Funnies'

The 79th Armoured Division commanded by Maj-General Sir Percy Hobart was affectionately known as 'the zoo'. It carried stocks of a number of specially developed or adapted tracked vehicle. These 'funnies' were available to formations of the 21st Army Group as required.

DD – Duplex Drive. Some 900 tanks were made amphibious for the D-Day landings by fitting a collapsible canvas screen around the top of the hull. They were also equipped with propellers.

Crab or Flail – This was a tank adapted for minefield clearance. It was fitted at the front with a chain flail which exploded mines in its path. Usually Sherman tanks.

Crocodile – Fitted with a flame thrower, the fuel for which was carried in a two-wheeled armoured trailer. Usually Churchill tanks.

Kangeroo – A tank with its turret removed and used for conveying troops.

Water Buffalo or Alligator – Not a tank but a specially designed tracked amphibious vehicle, capable of carrying personnel or a Jeep.

AVRE – Assault Vehicle Royal Engineers. They took a number of forms:
1. Fitted with a mortar or 'petard' in place of a gun for use against concrete pillboxes and obstructions.
2. With a 'scissors bridge' mounted on the hull which, when unfolded, could span a short gap.
3. A fascine carrier with a bundle of wood mounted at the front which could be released to fill a crater or ditch.
4. 'Bobbin' track layer. A roll of metal mesh was carried and this could be unrolled to form a trackway over marshy fields.

DD tank with skirt down.

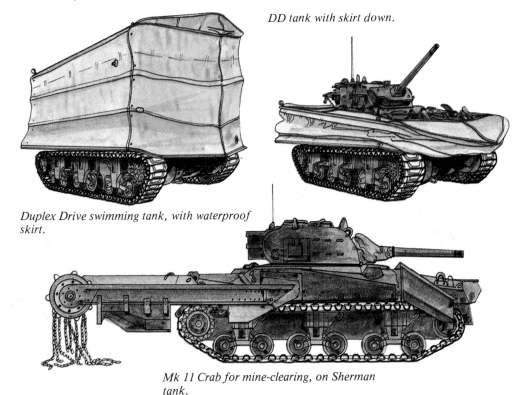

Duplex Drive swimming tank, with waterproof skirt.

Mk 11 Crab for mine-clearing, on Sherman tank.

unexpected heavy attack from German artillery but their strength was greatly depleted by the loss of some landing craft, with those rescued finding themselves on a return voyage to England. The 41st at Lion-sur-Mer also had some troubles but the main difficulty came when darkness fell and a mixed force of armour and infantry of the 21st Panzer Division succeeded in reaching the coast at Luc-sur-Mer, between the two Commandos, thus splitting the British/Canadian beaches. However, this threat was not to last, the Germans withdrawing as follow-up landings progressed.

The most easterly of the invasion beaches was SWORD with the British 3rd Division landing at La Brèche. This was a comparatively built-up area and the Germans had taken the opportunity of converting the houses into defensive bunkers. This was the only area where the Allies met Naval opposition in the shape of three E Boats – in this action the Norwegian destroyer *Svenner* was torpedoed and sunk.

The landing was expensive in terms of casualties and equipment but by 0900 hours La Brèche had been taken and an advance made inland towards Coleville.

Finally, the town of Ouistreham on the eastern extremity of SWORD had to be taken and this was achieved in the early afternoon by No. 4 Commando and two troops of French Commandos.

D-Day ended and history had been made; many gallant men had died but the number was less than expected. To all who took part it was a momentous day; they would never, could never, see its like again.

'On the ground' quote

'My worst memory of the 'funnies' was having to pass a Crocodile one dark night. It had hit a very substantial land mine and was laying ablaze on its side in a ditch. A crew member had been trapped underneath and was still conscious.

I had to pass that way again the following morning and the poor man's fate was all too evident.'

V. Battle of Normandy

'As a result of the D-Day operations, a foothold has been gained on the continent of Europe.'
General Sir Bernard Montgomery's report,
June 6, 1944
'On the ground' quote

'It must have been the second or third evening after the landing that we were given an hour or two of relaxation with a session of Housey-Housey in a mess tent erected in a field alongside an orchard. This was a game now universally known as Bingo and was, probably still is, the only gambling permitted in the British Army.

Our CSM was the caller and his shouts of "legs eleven" and "ducks on a pond" had a strange ring of reassurance in this alien place. We were much more used to him calling out "That Man There!" or "I'm standing on what's supposed to be your short and curlies!".

But the memory of that evening, on which we were given our first ration of beer, is of the wasps from the orchard. Going back to the tin mug after an "eyes down" to find five or six wasps floating in the beer.'

British Infantry Equipment.

US Infantry Equipment.

German leather Infantry Equipment.

British infantrymen, 50th (Northumbrian) Div.

POST D-DAY – JUNE 1944 After D-Day the bridgehead is gradually expanded and the pockets of German resistance cleared and here numbers of Germans are taken prisoner. American bombers fly south to attack the enemy concentrations.

POST D-DAY – JUNE 1944 Nurses, doctors and orderlies of the Royal Army Medical Corps tend the wounded in front line dressing stations, and in Field Hospitals behind the lines, reducing the number of fatal casualties through prompt action and modern techniques, particularly blood transfusions and the use of new drugs. A chaplain comforts a severly wounded soldier.

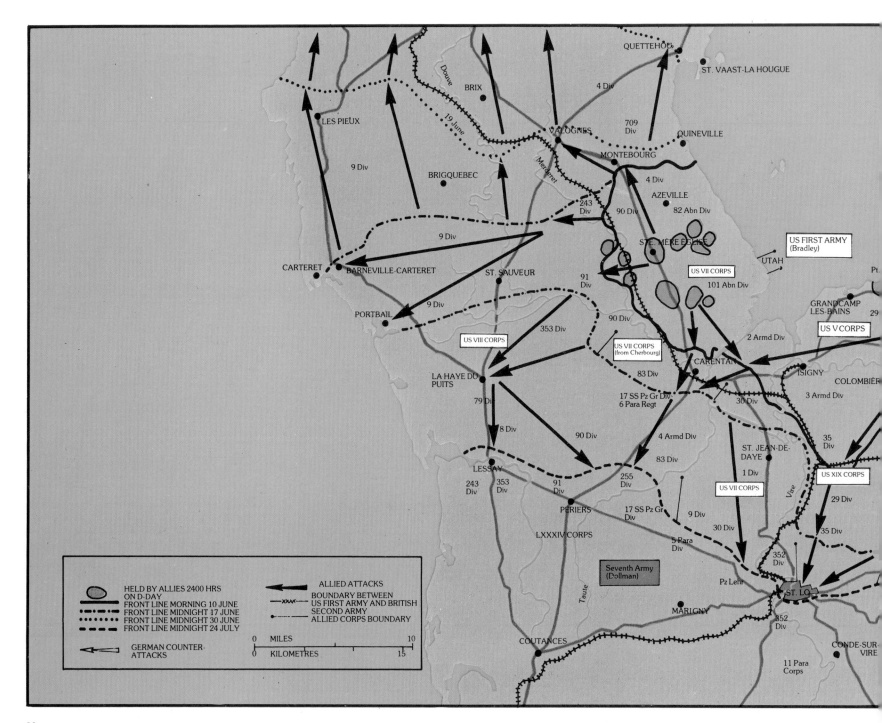

QUETTEHOU

ST. VAAST-LA HOUGUE

Douve

BRIX

4 Div

19 June

VALOGNES

709
Div

QUINEVILLE

MONTEBOURG

LES PIEUX

Merderet

9 Div

4 Div

BRIGQUEBEC

AZEVILLE

243
Div

82 Abn Div

90 Div

9 Div

STE. MÈRE ÉGLISE

US FIRST ARMY
(Bradley)

CARTERET

BARNEVILLE-CARTERET

ST. SAUVEUR

91
Div

US VII CORPS

UTAH

101 Abn Div

GRANDCAMP
LES-BAINS

29

9 Div

90 Div

PORTBAIL

US VIII CORPS

353 Div

US VII CORPS
(from Cherbourg)

2 Armd Div

US V CORPS

CARENTAN

83 Div

ISIGNY

COLOMBIÈR

LA HAYE DU
PUITS

17 SS Pz Gr Div
6 Para Regt

30 Div

3 Armd Div

79 Div

8 Div

90 Div

4 Armd Div

83 Div

ST. JEAN-DE-
DAYE

35
Div

US XIX CORPS

LESSAY

243
Div

353
Div

91
Div

255
Div

1 Div

US VII CORPS

Vire

29 Div

PERIERS

17 SS Pz Gr
Div

9 Div

30 Div

35 Div

LXXXIV CORPS

5 Para
Div

352
Div

Seventh Army
(Dollman)

Pz Lehr

ST. LO

Taute

MARIGNY

352
Div

COUTANCES

CONDE-SUR-
VIRE

11 Para
Corps

HELD BY ALLIES 2400 HRS
ON D-DAY
FRONT LINE MORNING 10 JUNE
FRONT LINE MIDNIGHT 17 JUNE
FRONT LINE MIDNIGHT 30 JUNE
FRONT LINE MIDNIGHT 24 JULY

GERMAN COUNTER-
ATTACKS

ALLIED ATTACKS

BOUNDARY BETWEEN
US FIRST ARMY AND BRITISH
SECOND ARMY
ALLIED CORPS BOUNDARY

0   MILES   10
0   KILOMETRES   15

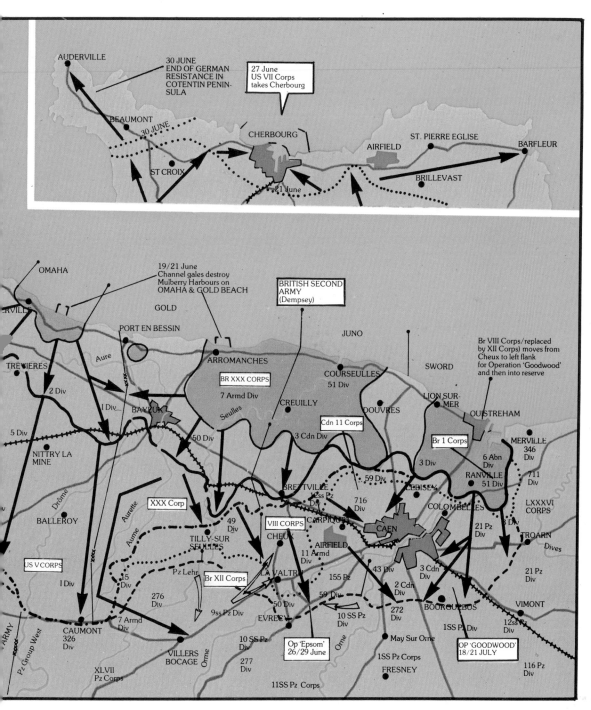

Battle Code Names

BLUECOAT The 8th and 30th British Corps offensive against Vire starting on 30th July 1944.
DAUNTLESS The 30th Corps part in EPSOM battle. 25 June 1944.
EPSOM Battle to cross the Oden and Orne rivers SW of Caen, involving British 2nd Army. 26 June-1 July 1944.
GOODWOOD Attack SE of Caen by British 2nd Army, 18-21 July 1944.
JUPITER Attack towards upper Orne by VIII Corps, 10 July 1944.
TOTALIZE Phase I attack towards Falaise by 1st Canadian Army, 8-11 August 1944.
TRACTABLE Phase II attack towards Falaise by 1st Canadian Army, 14-18 August 1944.

Commands

AEAF Allied Air Forces under command of Air Chief Marshal Leigh-Mallory.
ANCXF Allied Naval Forces under command of Admiral Ramsey.
COSSAC Chief of Staff to the Supreme Allied Command.
EXFOR MAIN General Eisenhower's SHAEF headquarters.
EXFOR TAC General Montgomery's 21st Army Group Headquarters.
TROOPERS LONDON War Office, London.
UNITY Combined Headquarters.

Among the first vehicles to come ashore were jeeps fitted as stretcher ambulances. These were part of the services for the wounded that ranged from Field Ambulance units and Advanced Field Dressing Stations, as part of each formation, to complete Field Hospitals which were established as the beach-head was strengthened.

The work of the medical orderlies and stretcher bearers at company level was impressive. In the thick of battle, under cover of a white flag with a red cross, white helmets and armbands, these men went about tending friend and foe alike and removing them to the Royal Army Medical Corps doctors at the Advanced Field Dressing Stations.

It was not uncommon to see British or American medical staff working with their German

POST D-DAY – JUNE 1944 A few days after the landings King George VI, Winston Churchill and Field Marshal Brooke tour the beaches with Generals Eisenhower and Montgomery. In the background is the prefabricated Mulberry harbour.

JUNE/JULY 1944 The Allies fight in the heavily wooded Normandy 'bocage' to enlarge their bridgehead. The German tanks and guns are in a strong position; well sheltered and defended behind thick banks and hedges. A series of offensives draw the German Armour towards the British preparatory to a decisive American breakthrough in the west.

counterparts, who had come in as prisoners. Of course, casualties were inevitable but it is fair to say that both sides respected the sign of the red cross and the non-combatant status of those who wore it.

The MULBERRY harbour design and provision had been the responsibility of the Royal Navy. These artificial harbours, originally suggested by Winston Churchill, had been undergoing construction throughout 1943.

Two complete harbours were required, one for OMAHA and the other for GOLD off Arromanches. The outer breakwaters, known as GOOSEBERRIES were, in fact, merchant ships deliberately scuttled and sunk so as to provide calm waters within the harbour. The piers, or unloading roadways, floated and went up and down with the tide.

160 tugs and 10,000 men were needed to assemble the two harbours at their locations, and, unfortunately, the OMAHA MULBERRY was only to be operated for a few days, becoming wrecked in a gale that started on 19 June.

The GOLD MULBERRY, however, continued in service for many months, and the Americans found they could quite satisfactorily beach cargo ships on UTAH for unloading into trucks.

The battle for Villers-Bocage was typical of actions in the early days of the invasion.

Men of the 7th Armoured Division – the 'Desert Rats' – had just occupied the small town of some 1,000 inhabitants when the Germans opened fire. The British tanks in the lanes up to the town were hull-down behind hedges but each time they moved they were fired on. The action was going badly for the British and those in the town were compelled to withdraw, leaving a squadron of tanks outflanked by the enemy infantry.

Fire was coming from all directions and German anti-tank 88mm guns made sure that an English tank could turn a corner only at its peril. As reported by War Correspondent Alan Morehead, in his excellent personal account of the campaign, *Eclipse*:

'At this stage the Germans were far ahead of us in using the country. Their infantry smothered themselves in leaves and branches. They crawled up to the forward positions on their stomachs. They never showed themselves. Whole platoons of soldiers would lie themselves into the leafy branches of trees, and there they would wait silently for hours, even days, until they got the chance of a shot . . . You had to be ready to jump for the ditches at every daylight hour . . .'

At last it was decided that Villers-Bocage should be bombed, and bombed it was: twenty minutes of hell made it a ruinous pile of bricks. Again the British troops went forward, only to be met by the same opposition – the Germans had simply taken to the fields when the air raid started! The devastation was in vain, and it was to be days before the town was eventually retaken.

From the Allies' viewpoint, actions such as Villers-Bocage were the negative side of June 1944, before the breakthrough that was inevitably to come.

AEC Matador, 4x4 Medium Artillery Tractor.

Diamond T 6x4, M20 Tank Transport Prime Mover.   *Sherman tank mounted on 40-ton trailer.*

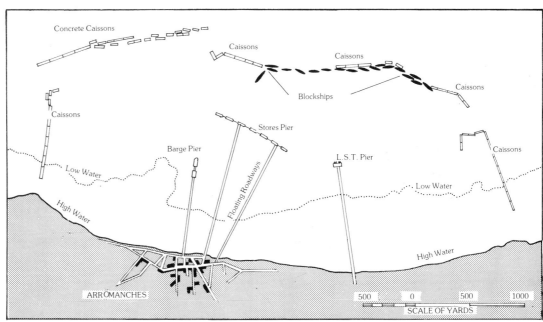

Plan of the pre-fabricated Mulberry Harbour, built to provide calm waters and floating piers for landing supplies at Arromanches on Gold Beach area. Successfully used for many months after its construction.

JULY 1944 The battle for Caen was the last all-British battle fought in Europe and the first for more than 200 years. Never again could sufficient Empire troops be gathered under one command to fight a battle alone.

Over 2,000 tons of bombs fell on Caen prior to the attack of the Allied ground forces.

At 0430 hours on 8 July I Corps began its all-out offensive with three divisions – 3rd Canadian, 3rd British and 59th (Staffordshire), supported by two armoured brigades. The Canadians were on the right and by dusk their tanks were on the western outskirts of the city, the 3rd British was into the north east corner, and the 59th was closing in from the north.

The following morning the 3rd Canadian and 3rd British met in the dock area, although the town was not completely cleared for some days.

'On the ground' quote

'After the bombing and fall of Caen we were stationed for a little while in what had been a small German Army hutted camp, the huts made of chipboard – the first time I'd seen this sort of material.

In Caen itself all was devastated. There really was a smell of death in the air, but here and there were pockets where buildings had survived; I remember a particular pen shop stocked with Mont Blanc fountain pens. But most of all, I remember the Cathedral where the "padre" had set up an "English Church". Here was a notice on the door to the effect:

"We want this to be used as a power house where

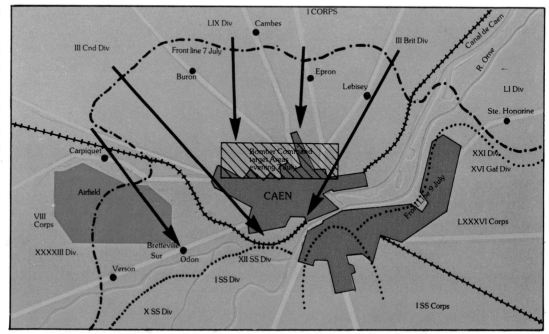

The capture of Caen in the operation by combined British and Canadian forces, 7-9 July 1944.

*JULY 1944 After a heavy air bombardment on the German positions, the 1st
U.S. Army under General Bradley break out near St. Lô. They overrun much of
Brittany and attempt to envelop the German 7th Army in Normandy.*

the spirit can be revived and refreshed to face the
struggles of life.''

*I copied it in my prayer book but this was destroyed
when a mortar bomb fell on our kit and I can't be sure
if the quote is correct!'*

The object of Operation GOODWOOD was to gain
the high ground on either side of the Caen-Falaise road
and to establish three armoured divisions, the 7th,
11th and Guards, at intervals of nine or ten miles. In
the early hours of 18 July the attack started with an
artillery barrage coupled with the effect of over 2,000
bombers of the Allied Air Forces. The result was five
miles of complete devastation and yet, as the 11th
Armoured Division historian tells us, 'beyond and
beside these fated acres the enemy waited beside his
guns'.

Around the village of Bourguebus, some five miles
south of Caen and to the east of the Falaise road, the
11th Armoured ran into particularly ferocious anti-
tank artillery fire and here this Division alone lost over
100 tanks in the first day of the operation.

The result was a static situation and, by the third
day, when the heavens opened and the scarred land
turned into a sea of mud, the scene was akin to a
Flanders field of a quarter of a century before.

What GOODWOOD did achieve was the clearing of

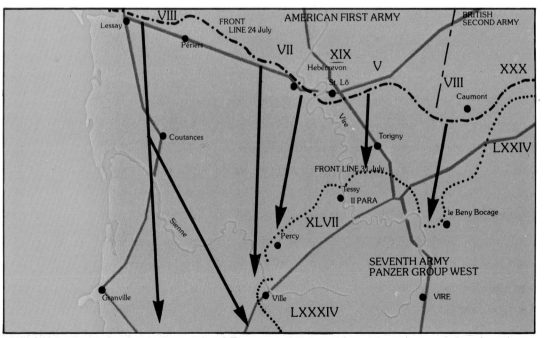

The breakout between 24-31 July with six allied corps advancing on a broad front; west, south and south-east.

AUGUST 1944 Completing the encirclement of the enemy, the First Canadian Army begins a southward offensive towards Falaise. Tanks are stripped of turrets and are used as improvised armoured personnel carriers.

The German 7th Army makes an unsuccessful westward counter attack towards Mortain, but fails to dislodge the Americans. Trapped in the Falaise pocket, it is virtually destroyed by fighter bombers, with 10,000 Germans killed and 50,000 captured. Rocket firing Typhoons attack transport and armour.

*THE ROAD TO VICTORY After Normandy has been retaken, bereaved
members of the French resistance watch British Infantrymen advancing
eastwards across Europe, where eight months of hard fighting still lie ahead
before the Allies win the war.*

German pockets of resistance from Caen's eastern and
southern suburbs and the strengthening of the Orne
bridgehead; objectives that had been planned for the
first day of the invasion and which were vital for the
subsequent thrust through France.

Operation COBRA was to start on 25 July near
Hebecrevon, west of St Lo, initially with a heavy
attack by bombers supported by ground artillery. The
bombardment was followed by the American VII
Corps attacking with three infantry divisions. Once
the flanks had been secured, two armoured divisions
and a motorised infantry division were to pass
through, driving west and south-east.

The bombardment began at 0940 hours and
unfortunately some shells fell on the American lines,
killing about 600 of the troops waiting to go into
action.

The US Infantry advanced at 1100 hours and at their
first objective, Hebecrevon, they met with strong
opposition and it was midnight before they achieved
success. In other areas resistance was quickly
overcome.

The armoured formations advanced as planned and
by the 31 July the troops of the German Seventh Army
had been driven back along a front: Villedien, Percy,
Tessy and le Beny Bocage.

Operation TOTALIZE and the subsequent battle in
the Falaise Pocket was probably the most decisive
action in Normandy after D-Day. Considerable forces
of German armour were attacking the Westerly
columns of Americans after their break-out in
Operation COBRA.

The attack began on 7 August, with General
Simmonds's II Canadian Corps, reinforced by the
British 51st (Highland) Division, 33rd Armoured
Brigade and the 1st Polish Armoured Division – newly
arrived in France.

An innovation of this operation was the use of
improvised armoured troop carriers called the
'unfrocked priests' or 'holy rollers' – originally, they
had been self-propelled field guns known as Priests
and were used on D-Day. Subsequently, they had been
replaced by British 25 pounders. With their guns
removed they made ideal troop carriers.

The plan for battle was for the 51st Division and
33rd Armoured Brigade to open the attack to the east
of the Falaise road, and 2nd Canadian Division and
2nd Canadian Armoured Brigade to attack the west.
Later the 1st Polish and 4th Canadian Armoured
Divisions were to pass through to attack Potigny and
Falaise areas.

The target area for the operation, from La Hogue to

the Orne was occupied by I SS Panzer Corps and the
89th Infantry Division, behind which was the 12th SS
Panzer Division. Also in the area were III Flak Corps
and the 272nd Division.

2300 hours 7 August, was the moment for the start
of a thousand bomber raid by Bomber Command.
Half an hour later the infantry and tanks advanced
towards the bombs. As the columns progressed, so a
barrage of 360 guns was opened up in front of them,
lifted 200 yards every two minutes to allow the assault
to continue.

By daybreak several villages had been captured. But
the Germans fought back fiercely and much of the
success must be attributed to the air attacks made by
Typhoons, Spitfires and Mustangs of the Second
Tactical Air Force.

The Battle of Normandy ended on 27 August 1944.
There were other battles, both victories and defeats, to
come before the war in Europe ended in May 1945:
Arnhem, The Scheldt Estuary, The Ardennes, the
hard winter and then The Rhine Crossing – itself a
remarkable amphibious operation – and then the final
tiring weeks of driving into the heart of Germany
before the lights of Europe were again turned on.

Command of the Allied Expeditionary Force 6th June 1944

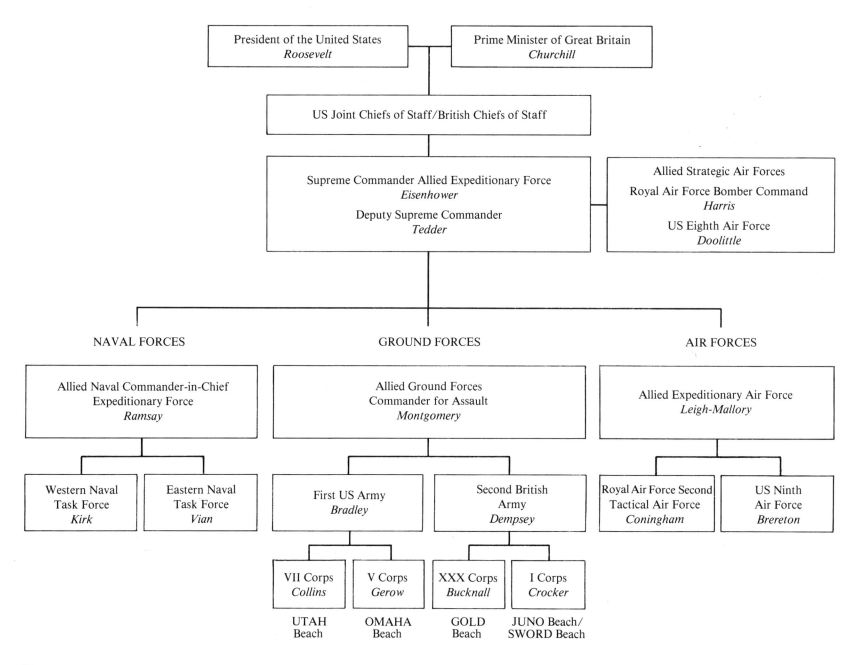

German Command in the West 6th June 1944

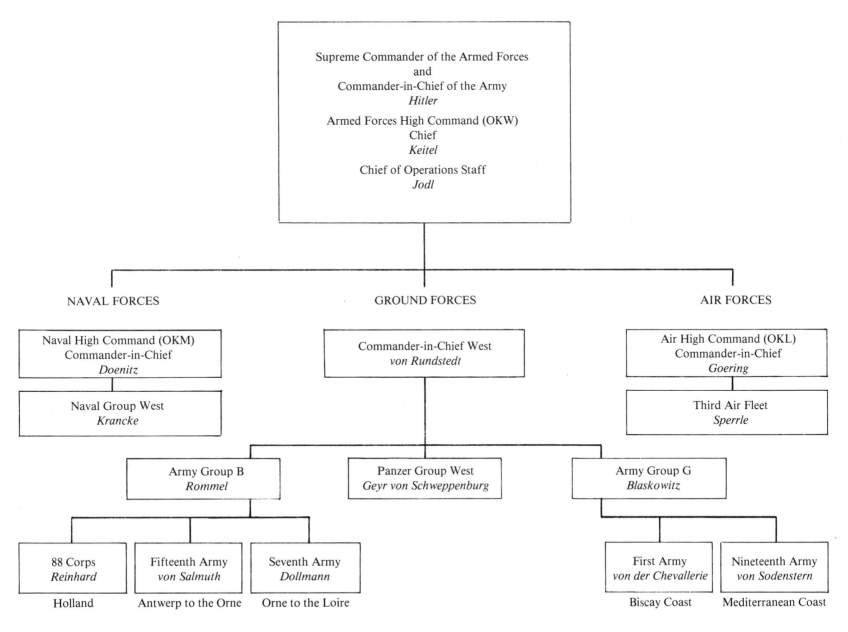

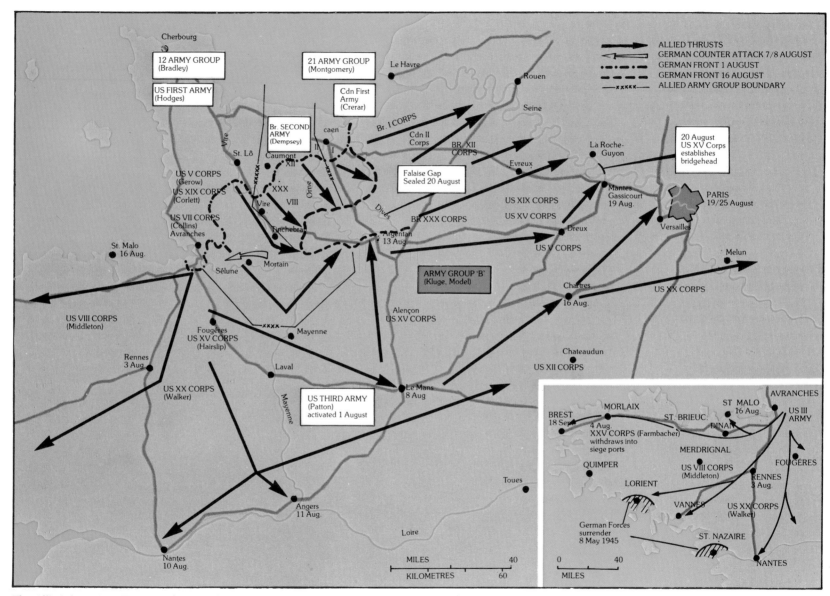

The Allied thrust into Europe. The map shows how the front line changed, hinging on Caen, between 1-16 August. German Forces contained in what was known as the Falaise Pocket were sealed in on 20 August, the same day as the US XV Corps established a bridgehead across the river Seine.

Designation of Landing Craft as close-support weapons used in Operation NEPTUNE

Type of Craft		Western Task Force	Eastern Task Force
LCG(L)	– Landing Craft Gun (Large)	9	16
	Armament – Two 4.7″ naval guns; 2 to 7 30mm Oerlikon AA guns		
LCT(R)	– Landing Craft Tank (Rocket)	14	22
	Armament – 800 to 1000 5″ HE rockets		
LCS(L)	– Landing Craft Support (Large)	0	14
	Armament – One 6 pdr/one 2 pdr gun in tank turret; 2.5″ machine guns; two 20mm Oerlikon AA guns; one 4″ smoke mortar		
LCS(M)	– Landing Craft Support (Medium)	2	24
	Armament – 2.5″ machine guns; one 4″ smoke mortar		
LCS(S)	– Landing Craft Support (Small)	36	0
	Armament – 24 rockets; 2.5 machine guns		
LCF	– Landing Craft Flak	11	18
	Armament – Alternative armament of four 2 pdrs & 8 Oerlikons/eight 2 pdrs & 4 Oerlikon guns		
LCA(H)	– Landing Craft Assault (Hedgerow)	0	45
	Armament – twenty-four 60lb Spigot bombs		
LCT(T)	– Landing Craft Tank, with temporary mounted armaments: Centaur tanks with 96mm howitzers, Sherman tanks with 75mm guns, self-propelled field guns or 17 pdr high-velocity guns for use against concrete defences.	26	103

Designations of Landing Ships and Craft Types

LSH – Landing Ship Headquarters. Used as command posts for commanders of all services with operations rooms, radio communication and accommodation for staff. Passenger liners were used for corps and divisional command.

LSI – Landing Ship Infantry. Passenger and cargo merchant ships were used for this purpose with assault landing craft carried in place of lifeboats.

LST – Landing Ship Tank. Ocean going vessels with bow doors and ramp. Either beached or unloaded while at anchor into LCTs or Rhino ferries. Some were used as Flight Direction Tenders, carrying RAF radar equipment. Others were later converted to carry railway locomotives and rolling stock.

LSC – Landing Ship Carrier. Used for ferrying landing craft. Several versions were in service:
LSD – Landing Ship Dock
LSG – Landing Ship Gantry
LSS – Landing Ship Stern-chute

LCI(L) – Landing Craft Infantry (Large). Two hundred of these craft took part in Neptune, each with a capacity of 200 men.

LCI(S) – Landing Craft Infantry (Small). Wooden-hulled with a capacity of 100 men.

LCT – Landing Craft Tank. Flat-bottomed with a drop-ramp to discharge three tanks or other vehicles.

LCA – Landing Craft Assault. An armoured craft with a capacity of 36 men, who landed by means of a ramp in the bow.

LCVP – Landing Craft Vehicle and Personnel. American version of British originated I CA. Without armour.

LCP – Landing Craft Personnel. Similar in size to LCVP but without ramp.

LCM – Landing Craft Mechanised. Could carry an 18-ton tank but was light enough to be lifted out of the water by a ship's derricks.

RHINO FERRY – A raft made up from steel pontoons and driven by a detachable propulsion unit.

Tanks engaged in operation OVERLORD

Allied

STUART — Armour 44mm (front), 25mm (sides), Armament 37mm Max speed 40 mph. Weight 12½-15 tons. Used for reconnaissance.

SHERMAN — Armour 76mm (front), 51mm (sides). Armament 75mm (some called 'Fireflies' with British units had 17 pdr.) some with US units 76mm. Max speed 24 mph. Weight 30-32 tons.

CHURCHILL — Mks I to VI. Armour 90mm (front), 76mm (sides). Armament 75mm (some with 6 pdr). Max speed 15 mph. Weight 37 tons.

CHURCHILL — Mk VII. Armour 150mm (front). 95mm (sides). Armament 75mm. Max speed 12 mph. Weight 41 tons. In service with flame thrower regiment of 79th Armoured Division and 34th Tank Brigade.

CROMWELL — Armour 75mm (front), 63mm (sides). Armament 75mm. Max speed 40 mph. Weight 27 tons.

German

MARK IV — Armour 80mm (front), 30mm (sides), Armament 75mm Kwk 40. Max speed 25 mph. Weight 25 tons.

MARK V (PANTHER) Armour 100mm (front), 45mm (sides), Armament 75mm Kwk 42. Max speed 34 mph. Weight 45 tons. The JAGDPANTHER version had front armour of 80mm.

MARK VIE (TIGER) Armour 100mm (front), 80mm (sides). Armament 88mm KwK 36. Max speed 23 mph. Weight 54 tons.

MARK VIB (TIGER) Armour 180mm (front), 80mm (sides). Armament 88mm KwK 43. Max speed 25 mph. Weight 68 tons. JAGDTIGER version had front armour of 250mm.

Allied tanks also had two light machine guns.
German tanks also had up to three machine guns.

The Three Surrenders

4th May, 1945 The first surrender took place at Montgomery's Tactical H.Q. on Luneburg Heath, where Admiral von Friedburg and other representatives of the German High Command signed an armistice surrendering all German forces in North-West Germany, Denmark, Holland and Dunkirk.

7th May, 1945 The second surrender, at Eisenhower's H.Q. in Rheims, took place in the presence of representatives of the United States, Great Britain, the Soviet Union and France. Jodl and von Friedeburg, acting for Doenitz, signed an instrument which provided for the unconditional surrender of all German forces on all fronts.

8th May, 1945 In Berlin, the final act of unconditional surrender was signed at 00.16 in the early morning in a building formerly housing the Pioneer College of the Wehrmacht in the suburb of Karlshorst.

The German delegates –
Generalfeldmarschall Keitel, Chief of the German Army High Command, Generaladmiral von Friedeburg, Commander-in-Chief of the German Navy, and Generaloberst Stumpf of the Luftwaffe – were ushered at midnight into a room draped with the British, American, Russian and French flags.
In the presence of Marshal Zhukov, Keitel was asked by Air Chief Marshal Tedder whether he understood the terms of unconditional surrender. On replying in the affirmative, he, von Friedeburg and Stumpf signed for Germany, the Allied signatories being Marshal Zhukov, for the Soviet High Command, and Air Chief Marshal Tedder, for the Allied Expeditionary Force. Lieutenant-General Spaatz and General de Lattre de Tassigny also signed as witnesses.

Forces engaged in Overlord

The scale of operations and size of the forces involved in the invasion of Europe are summarised with great efficiency in Major L. F. Ellis's book *Victory in the West Volume I: The Battle of Normandy.*

. . . The armada which was to put the armies ashore and to sustain them on the Continent included over twelve hundred fighting vessels of all kinds, over four thousand assault ships and craft and about sixteen hundred merchant ships and ancillary vessels.

. . . By the time the campaign opened there would be gathered in the United Kingdom Allied armies totalling over three and a half million men. The British Army would number nearly one and three-quarter millions, Dominion forces one hundred and seventy-five thousand, the United States army and air forces a million and a half and other national contingents nearly forty-four thousand. There would be some thirteen thousand aircraft in the country [Britain], including over four thousand bombers and some five thousand fighters . . . and about three thousand five hundred gliders.

The German occupying forces prior to D-Day have been numbered at about one million four hundred thousand. Naval surface vessels based at ports on Channel and Atlantic coasts from Ijmuiden in the north, to Bayonne in the south, comprised five destroyers, thirty-four motor torpedo boats, three hundred and nine mine-sweepers, one hundred and sixteen patrol vessels and forty-two artillery barges. The German air force strength at the time comprised eight hundred and ninety one aircraft, of which four hundred and ninety seven were serviceable.

THE COST

Land Forces Casualties 6 June – 31 August 1944

British and Canadian Armies
16,138 killed, 58,594 wounded, 9,093 missing.

US Army Casualties
20,838 killed, 94,881 wounded, 10,128 missing.

TOTAL of 209,672 casualties

German casualty figures for this period have been estimated at about 400,000, half of whom were taken prisoners-of-war.

Air Forces Casualties

RAF 2nd Tactical Air Force and Air Defence GB
1,036 killed or missing. 829 aircraft lost.

RAF Bomber Command
6,761 killed or missing. 983 aircraft lost

RAF Coastal Command
382 killed or missing. 224 aircraft lost

US 8th Air Force
7,167 killed or missing. 1,168 aircraft lost

US 9th Air Force
1,369 killed or missing. 897 aircraft lost

TOTAL for Allied Air Forces, 16,714 air crew killed or missing.

BIBLIOGRAPHY

Battle of Hastings and the Bayeux Tapestry

Ashley, M. *William I*
Burne, Lt-Col A. H. *The Battlefields of England*
Creasy, Sir E. *Creasy's Fifteen Decisive Battles*
Dixon, P. *Barbarian Europe*
Douglas, D. *The Norman Achievement*
Freeman-Grenville, G. S. P. *Atlas of British History*
Fuller, Maj-Gen J. F. C. *Decisive Battles of the Western World*
Gibbs-Smith, Charles H. *The Bayeux Tapestry*
Lemmon, Lt-Col Charles H. *The Field of Hastings*
Lester, G. A. *The Anglo-Saxons*
Lytton, Lord *Harold 'Last of the Saxon Kings'*
Page, R. I. *Life in Anglo-Saxon England*
Reader's Digest *Heritage of Britain*
Reader's Digest *The Past All Around Us*
Stenton, Sir F. *The Bayeux Tapestry*
Thorpe, Lewis *The Bayeux Tapestry and the Norman Invasion*
Tryckare, T. *The Vikings*
Wise, T. *Saxon, Viking and Norman*
Wise, T. *1066. Year of Destiny*
Wood, T. *Age of Chivalry*

The Invasion of Europe and the Overlord Embroidery

Belfield & Essame *The Battle for Normandy*
Bradley, Gen Omar *A Soldier's Story*
Churchill, Winston S. *The Second World War*
Clay, E. W. *Path of the 50th*
Darby & Cunliffe *A Short Story of 21 Army Group*
Edwards, Kenneth *Operation Neptune*
Eisenhower, Dwight D *Crusade in Europe*
Ellis, Maj L. F. *Victory in the West – Vol I*

Fergusson, Bernarn *The Watery Maze*
Gale, Sir Richard *The Sixth Airborne Division in Normandy*
Guderian, Gen Heinz *Panzer Leader*
de Guingand, Maj-Gen Sir Francis *Operation Victory*
Hickey, Michael *Out of the Sky*
Howarth, David *Dawn of D-DAY*
Hunter & Brown *Battle Coast*
Jaconsen & Rohwer *Decisive Battles of World War II*
Leahy, Fleet Admiral William D. *I Was There*
Liddel Hart, Sir B. H. *History of the Second World War*
The Other Side of the Hill
Loulton, J. L. *Haste to the Battle*
McElwee, William *The Battle of D-DAY*
Martin H. G. *History of the 15th Scottish Division*
Montgomery, Field Marshal Viscount *Normandy to the Baltic*
Morgan, Lt-Gen Frederick *Overture to Overlord*
North, John *North-West Europe 1944-5*
Norton, Maj G. *The Red Devils*
Otway, Lt-Col T. B. H. *Airborne Forces – The Second World War*
Ramsey, Admiral *The Assault Phase of the Normandy Landings*
Ryan, Cornelius *The Longest Day*
St George Saunder, Hilary *The Green Beret*
The Red Beret
Shire, W. L. *The Rise & Fall of the Third Reich*
Smith, Lt-Gen Walter Bedell *Eisenhower's Six Great Decisions*
Stacey, Col C. P. *The Canadian Army, 1939-45*
Thompson, R. W. *D-Day*
US War Department *To Cherbourg Omaha Beachhead*
Westphal, Den Siegried *The German Army in the West*
Wilmott, Chester *The Struggle for Europe*